P9-CFX-022

parameters of learning

perspectives in higher education today

WILLIAM JAMES McKEEFERY

SOUTHERN ILLINOIS UNIVERSITY PRESS

Carbondale and Edwardsville

FEFFER & SIMONS, INC.   *London   and   Amsterdam*

contents

list of figures

foreword

COLLEGE and university educators predict radical internal changes during the 1970s, and at the same time students demand it. The opportunity appears greater than at any time in the past for major improvements in the quality and amount of learning that takes place.

A watershed period is developing in American higher education, and the need for measurement of the consequences of learning experiences has never been more critical. Fortunately, our creative society has provided dozens of ways to preserve knowledge and dozens of ways in which knowledge can be studied and transmitted from one generation to the next. Unfortunately, our analyses of these resources have often been inadequate, and measurement techniques have had limited validity.

A recent, very significant national study revealed that the most desirable of thirty-five important and possible higher education developments of the seventies would be: "Breakthroughs in understanding the human learning process [which] will lead to major improvements in instructional methods at the college level."

The same group of over two thousand persons—made up of institutional members of the American Council on Education, chapter heads of the American Association of University Professors, leaders in the National Student Association, and principal members of the Association of Governing Boards of Colleges and Universities—felt that desirable as this outcome might be, it was very close to the bottom in terms of the probability of its happening. (*The Future Academic Community: Continuity and Change,* edited by John Caffrey. Washington: American Council on Education, 1969.) Thus, promising methods of analysis, which can make its happening more probable, are of considerable significance in this strategic decade.

Parameters of Learning presents a refreshing approach to this important subject. Dr. McKeefery establishes the parameters and examines learning in a way which is extremely useful and somewhat different from more ordinary methods of description. Melding of scientific and humanistic cultures must take place through the work of persons who have had a depth of experience in both cultures. The author's background, both as an engineering scientist and as a successful scholar in the field of philosophy, provides him with a special and needed understanding of the "two cultures." It is a particularly valuable attribute for one who would "uncover" the subject of "learning" for needy but often unwilling members of the higher education community.

He has identified the parameters for learning on seven different scales, and his purpose is to observe the present location of some of the "constants" and how they might change. He also examines the effective technology and suggests some of the ways in which it will have a permanent impact on higher education. Finally, he proposes that some

of the long-established constants in higher education may
be changed rather dramatically through new relationships
which are opened up through careful analysis of advanced
technology and learning tasks. Teaching by the basic lecture method of presentation originally was the only suitable method available. At the present time many alternatives are available, and careful choices can be made by
teachers and students regarding the best way in which
learning can be sought and achieved.

The crux of this brief but provocative and stimulating
book is a two-dimensional model based on seven characteristics which define the parameters of learning. The model
is limited because it applies primarily to what Dr.
McKeefery calls "middle length learning experiences, conducted in class groups as a part of organized instruction
toward a baccalaureate degree." However, he has included
comparative discussion of other ways of structuring the
opportunities for learning. The seven critical variables
which are defined in some detail are: 1] the people,   2]
the space,   3] the time,   4] the process,   5] the inputs,
6] the interactions, and   7] the outputs. These characteristics are on one axis or dimension of the model, and the
other dimension is the extent to which any one of these
given characteristics is present. As a result of the author's
experience there is a particularly interesting and useful
emphasis on the inputs, interactions, and outputs. With
increasing societal emphasis on "accountability" and "effectiveness of the college experience," in contrast to more
limited ideas of "quality" based primarily on static input
measures, higher education can well afford to consider very
carefully the interaction and output characteristics which
he has outlined.

Dr. McKeefery points out quite cogently the effects

which an active student voice may have in curriculum and teaching developments in the future. The further increase of a developing "adversary" system rather than the cooperative community of scholars could lead to greater tension. However, he sees the new factors as a genuine opportunity and a real resource if they are used to advantage. Greater innovation in teaching and learning could take place if the tension is treated creatively without breakdowns in communication between faculty and students.

For centuries teaching has been regarded as an art, and in the words of the author has developed a special "mystique." This is undoubtedly true. Now, the advantages of many additional forms of storage, retrieval and study of knowledge must be added. This little book, with its emphasis on the measurement of behavioral change resulting from learning experiences and its references to a continuous progress system of learning in higher education, provides a most interesting way for scholars in higher education to assess the framework in which students learn and, hopefully, their senior scholars also continue to learn.

Fred F. Harcleroad

15 April 1970
Iowa City, Iowa

preface

the educational dimensions

For centuries man has engaged in the learning process without much conscious thought to its dimensions. Of this scant attention, most has been directed to the progress of the student in a subject field. Custom has frowned upon innovation so that few teachers have ventured beyond the limits set by their predecessors. Within the well-worn pathways, dominated by the lecture technique and the classroom enclosure, most of the teaching situations in higher education have developed. These strictures, first imposed by lack of alternatives and now by choice, warrant careful reexamination.

Although teaching is as old as man, or at least as old as the efforts of man to better prepare his offspring for the rigors of the world which sapped most of his energy, the authoritarian hand has laid heavily upon it. One wonders that as much good came from the experience as its graduates later proclaimed. One is also led to speculate on why able students circumvented the imposed system and managed to learn in spite of it.

Apparently this student initiative was an important factor in the formation of the medieval university. Bands of students sought out able teachers, commandeered towns and entered into contracts with teachers for specific learning outcomes. From the German university came the graduate school devoted to research. The student was no longer the first concern of the teacher, but the advancement of knowledge and the power of the faculty grew. This power has continued until the present so that the collective resources of a faculty can manage research pursuits and still effectively handle a student body ten to twenty times its size. This social counterpoise has not been seriously challenged until recent campus confrontations. The nature and fury of these incidents may cause a reexamination of the delegation of faculty prerogatives to administrators acting on their behalf but unable to protect all interests simultaneously.

Into this teacher-dominated environment has come technology and with it a host of commercial competitors. These recent rips in the fabric of tradition give pause but are no more threatening nor dramatically different than the circumstances that created the university itself. Frequent articles criticize current teaching practice and also criticize the university itself as obsolete.

Today the adversary system replaces the cooperative relationship between students and teachers. The teaching process itself may soon become a contest between those who seek innovation now possible with technology and those who seek collective associations striving for uniform procedures, minimum standards and reduced work loads. Almost everyone today from students to the governor wants a larger voice in the management of higher education.

the media invasion

Until recently only a few classroom experiences were enriched by the procedures made possible with media. Because their use is so recent and because of rapid changes now taking place, the student population is more easily adapted to media approaches than those who teach. For example, it is possible to find more students than faculty on a campus who know how to solve problems on the computer. It is also likely that the next generation of students will have greater facility with laser beams than the present young computer wizards. If it is true that students bring innovations to the classroom more quickly than teachers, the hope may lie in having the student's voice more fully heard in faculty councils. This generation lag with respect to the adoption of new technologies may lead to rethinking of a teacher-dominated environment.

There are currently on the market more than one thousand kinds of electronic devices to assist the teacher. To avoid being overwhelmed, one campus uses the strategy of getting wider faculty consent and then limiting the size of the venture until its worth is demonstrated. It is all too easy for a single faculty member to equip commonly-used classroom space with a device that he alone likes. Should he leave the institution, no one else cares to use these items. More important than innovation is the careful analysis of present procedures. The purpose of this study is not to pass judgment upon teaching methods, old or new, but to look at them analytically by finding their common elements, their differences, and the wide range of alternatives possible.

To cite the burst of technology is only to raise the larger questions of directions and purpose in higher education.

Many innovations do not involve technology, such as team teaching, nongraded schools, continuous progress and flexible scheduling. A great many do, such as closed circuit television, learning carrels, and computer-aided instruction. Large investments by equipment manufacturers suggest a substantial long-term market. Teachers have resisted marketing blandishments for their own reasons, but not all of the equipment was useful nor was the software well developed. Teachers are wary of equipment that is not foolproof and/or simple to operate. The overhead projector enjoys wide acceptance because the teaching materials are easily prepared, and the equipment is simple to use. The movie projector never enjoyed these advantages. This illustrative problem may be only temporary. More and more equipment will be designed for a "hands on" use by the teacher, and the keyboard of the computer may become as familiar as the dial on the telephone. Perfection of equipment will only sharpen the basic question of its contribution to the learning process.

Some of the devices made available to higher education are little more than gimmicks. Yet only a small fraction of a faculty use them after a period of time. Most lack a backup system in case of any malfunction, and some require considerable time to prepare materials. Because of these experiences, somewhat painful to institutions, more careful scrutiny is now given to both hardware and software. It is likely that federal assistance for instructional equipment will require careful thought by the proposing committee and broad concurrence from the faculty.

In reviewing the present patterns of teaching, new factors to consider are society's demands on higher education, a new clientele characterized by a vocal minority, and a different set of student inputs than the previous genera-

tion. Each of these can be seen as a resource. Public concern is important. Students are articulate and concerned.
Higher education appears prosperous and, like the airlines,
must handle a mass market. This can be a time of standard-
ization, efficiency, and jumbo jetlike classrooms. It could
be a time for innovation and increased individualization.
The time seems right to look at the total profile of teaching
experiences and to consider as many alternatives as possible
at a time when a wealthy nation decides to educate the
majority of its citizens beyond high school. Traditional
methods will not accomplish it using just six percent of
the gross national product. With technical assistance many
of the faculty resources can be more efficiently used. Many
more ideas should be tried.

the learning experience analyzed

Higher education needs a classification scheme for the varieties of higher education practice. From this matrix a description of the varieties of practice would first be derived
followed by the identification of parameters for learning.
These constants recurring in a wide range of teaching situations will be examined to see what reasons can be given
for them and how we might use them to predict further
developments in practice. If all the places along the dimensions of the learning process are examined, it is likely that
many more possibilities for expression exist than have ever
been tried. These gaps or untried places are of as much
interest as the well-worn pathways.

The learning experience is defined as the class experience in higher education lasting sufficiently long to identify the people and space involved as well as the inputs,
interactions, and outputs. This would normally be thought

to be the class hour; however, no narrow limits are being set. It is estimated that this definition would cover the bulk of what is now done as formal instruction in higher education. If the task of the university is to link the old and the young in the imaginative quest for learning, the formal experiences should take advantage of the wide variety of configurations possible. New avenues of practice have been opened up by technological advance, and there may also be areas of teaching value for which equipment does not now exist. If thinking is stretched toward these extremities, new possibilities may be grasped and old situations seen in new perspective.

A number of questions about the variety of teaching procedures come to mind. Are there many gaps in the total range of possible classroom procedures? Is there more equipment that can be meaningfully absorbed? Are there possibilities for new procedures that have not yet been tried or for which equipment does not exist? How much can students teach each other? Is the synthetic teacher an acceptable alternative? Will physical facilities built today be obsolete before the end of their predicted life-span? Is the end of the teacher shortage in sight? Not all of these questions can be answered by a taxonomy of learning procedures in higher education. These explorations will further shape the questions if not the answers.

It is hoped that a systematic review of the many ways learning can take place will stimulate some teachers to try new pathways. No mass movement is really expected. Much of the change we see in life takes the shape of a cold front with a narrow wedge of cold air lifting the air in its path. There is usually considerable turbulence at the point of the wedge. A small number of participants may be affected violently, and a few may try radically different procedures;

however, it is likely that twenty years from now many will use only a slightly modified lecture procedure. For those who are willing to stand at the edge of the storm where tension and trouble run high, there is hope that in the creation of tension there is also the excitement that develops significant change.

William James McKeefery

July 1, 1970
Blacksburg, Virginia

parameters of learning

seven categories of the learning experience

THE wide variety of practices carried out in higher education in pursuit of classroom learning has often been reviewed but seldom analyzed. The purpose now is to identify and arrange the essential elements of the hour-long classroom experience into a matrix with two dimensions: a categorical one grouping the elements and a quantitative one measuring the elements. Admittedly, other matrices could be constructed having three or even four dimensions. In this two-dimensional model one axis describes a series of seven characteristics or variables which together completely define the learning experience. This series includes the people, the space, the time, the process, the inputs, the interactions, and the outputs. The other dimension describes the extent to which a given characteristic is present. It is along this second axis that the parameters of frequently used teaching procedures are located. These constants once identified will be examined for their relevance to today's needs. Other locations on these continuums will then be explored for new and different procedures.

A comprehensive matrix of the total spectrum of the mid-length learning situation is necessary and useful. It is necessary because there is the tendency to think of only a few well-worn techniques as the total range of college classroom learning. The rapidly changing context of social values and the range of technological possibilities cause strains upon traditional techniques of teaching and prompt students to join in protest movements for a more relevant education. There is also the haunting hope that a better perspective will be obtained as present practice is looked at in the light or the gestalt of the total matrix. There is a challenge in attempting to make a model that is inclusive of a wide variety of styles and procedures and to make the matrix a useful diagnostic tool. If it can, on the one hand, contain a logical syntax akin to Bloom's *Taxonomy of Educational Objectives,* and on the other hand be a means of exploring new processes in new environments for which equipment and space may not yet be devised, it will have served a useful purpose.

Underlying the generality of the seven characteristics is a great complexity of human and technological interrelationships. The categories are a matter of convenience. Subscales describe these more complex relationships. For example, the professor is part of the person scale when giving a live lecture; however, he becomes an input when that same lecture is presented in televised form. The learning outcomes of the two lecture styles may be approximately the same; however, many subtle differences occur in the feedback possible, the use of professorial time, and the flexibility inherent in the live lecture. The cooler media approach of the television lecture in McLuhan's terms has a subtle effect on the audience different than that of a live lecturer. The human component is present to some extent in either case; however, subscales need be used to describe this difference.

Although this is an effort to look systematically and comprehensively at the mid-length learning situation, not all about it can be put down in quantitative terms nor are all the processes understood. From time immemorial, when the teaching of the young was a priestly function, a mystique has surrounded it. Some would call the teaching technique an art. Perhaps the reason for the mystique is to cover the practitioner's insufficiency or to keep the whole procedure from being regimented as had been the fate of the military.

There is, however, a case to be made for the learning experience as an art. It is a complex interaction of people, and when interactions are not fully understood, we plunge ahead and give to the whole our own flair. We become attached to these procedures and the styles demonstrated by our mentors and in turn teach them to others who follow.

One illustration of the mystique about teaching is the persistence of the ritual of direct contact with the teacher of the course. It is even suggested that the material cannot be learned apart from the personal attention of the teacher. Thus the student must sit in the class and take the tests when others do. Resistance to this separation is well entrenched, and it is next to impossible to find a reasonable equivalent by which a student can bypass a course on the basis of his proficiency. Another example of the art of teaching is the rich variety of idiosyncrasies such as surprise, suspense, scare, dramatic style, or an ambiance about the teacher that is genuine enough and students remember long after they have finished college work.

This concept of mystique is not unique to teaching. It shows up in the medical profession, law, and in public office. Mass media with its sharpened focus can build a specific image and give it wide dissemination. It can also be a ruthlessly honest medium and dispel an illusion about a person. The latter has been true with several political figures. A growing number of teacher-performers using television are very effective and have a wide appeal because their technique is a total personal impact. Certainly this is an acting skill, and the name art may be properly applied.

What has been described thus far are the several elements of the learning experience and the aura or ambiance that surrounds it. When looked at together it is hoped that a total configuration will manifest itself and provide new insights from this total impact. One element may be looked at in terms of another one or all together. The modes seen in this matrix can be used to construct other models or matrices. It is possible to be critical of the technique even while using it to look at present teaching practice and what it might become in the future. A procedure used for so long to convey the culture to so many develops a lore that must be carefully analyzed.

Why has the lecture remained the central means of informing the ongoing generation? Why has the larynx been used so exclusively? Are these mysteries, folklore, or proven techniques? An analysis of the complex forces at work in the lecture, as seen in the matrix may give some clues to its prevalence.

Certainly the lecture is in the midstream of cost ratios with a score of students to pay for a teacher's time. It balances the social weight of teacher and students who may be thought of as opposing authorities kept in dynamic balance. A minimum of preparation time is needed, and the notes can be reused. There is wide flexibility in technique through asking questions, calling for questions, and giving personal experiences. Little equipment is needed and it probably satisfies aggressive individuals who want to be approved. Perhaps it also lets the passive individual reside in his illusion about how effective he is. By the class structure and lecture, even an ineffective teacher is guaranteed a full class in required courses, and he may never know how good or how bad his teaching has been. The lecture technique will be discussed in more detail later. The purpose at this point is to illustrate the complexity in a learning mode of great popularity.

There are other models and model-makers of the teaching process. A profession as old as teaching has not been without its observers who attempted to analyze it. Aristotle sought, through a technique of classification, to organize the teaching experience. Edgar Dale and others have used topical and symbolic devices to segment the experience and graphically portray it. Thorndike gave it a set of laws and Dewey a functional concept for ideas. Perhaps the purpose of all models has been to make a complex process more explicit and thus more understandable and subject to change in terms of larger perspectives.

Among the characteristics considered in selecting a matrix for the mid-length learning experience in higher education are the following: 1] relevance to the current issues in higher education;   2] usefulness in a wide variety of circumstances;   3] adaptability to the changing conditions so it remains relevant;   4] simplicity in terms of its ease of application to known situations. In terms of outcomes it is hoped that this matrix will: 1] identify new areas that have not been tried or for which technical assistance has not been available;   2] search for a comprehensiveness that will show interrelationships;   3] become a source of critical evaluation itself.

One develops a matrix in much the same manner that one sends up a trial balloon. There is a large weight of tradition and a growing network of technology. How can a first attempt at a fit be made to draw off the greatest number of insights with the least number of non sequiturs?

Model-building is a worthy means of understanding the learning situation. Although the implications of a specific matrix is one purpose of this book, it is hoped this quest will stimulate others to find new and better models. If this model can lead to other sets of relationships on which others can build, it has served its purpose well. If a model can be used to develop a series of learning experiences in which the sought-for objectives are planned and the undesirable outcomes are reduced, then the use of models becomes a way to avoid expensive trial and error techniques.

The desire to locate most of the known educational experiences in a matrix may be viewed as a wish to do something about a tangled and amorphous learning situation. Those who analyze procedures in higher education find that the many follow a few all-too-familiar pathways. Those who stray from this small well-traveled segment of the known educational world are likely to be questioned by their colleagues.

There is another compelling reason to view what is happening in higher education analytically. Students are expressing their concern about the relevancy of their experience and have begun to use pressure tactics to be heard. The public through the legislature is already exercising financial restraint. A number of the newer junior colleges have developed physical plants to take advantage of a wide variety of learning experiences not possible in the older structures of established institutions. A message is being sent to those who will listen.

Still another reason to look at the total range of learning experiences is the rapid rise of bypass routes being opened by equipment manufacturers. These are often ingenious and workable techniques for which software is developed and specific outputs are guaranteed. This development will soon arrive at the point where those judging the output will say that it is as good as the colleges are doing. There may be many ways to achieve a specific objective, and a matrix is helpful in recognizing alternative paths.

If a matrix helps define the larger comprehensive activity then the middle-sized learning situation, primarily the classroom in higher education, may be seen in better perspective. This close scrutiny should take in the broad goals as well as the specific activities in the classroom. With respect to these overarching interests, thoughtful observers of teaching feel that the real purposes of those who engage in teaching in higher education are, in the order of priority, to: 1] advance knowledge in his particular field by study and research;   2] help recruit and develop those who will take on similar interests; 3] serve the broader community in terms of their own special field; and   4] provide some assistance in the general training of all students as it relates to their field of competency. That these priorities exist must be taken as a reality. In the last analysis these purposes are the ones to which the use of techniques will be fitted. Grading becomes a device that is used to encourage the most likely candidates for initiation to the subject-matter group. Grading also acts as sending one more stone crashing against the house of the student who may not survive the sifting process that higher education provides for business and industry.

It is not claimed that a model can do everything or even all that is necessary. Observers will interpret any model from different perspectives. Even the seven broad categories will have different demarcation points for some people. More important than the clarity of the model is its functional usefulness to point up where present practice is limited and where new practice is possible and needed. It is based on the assumption that there is more territory to explore than has been occupied to date.

It is also important to realize the limitations of a model. It applies to the middle-length learning experience in higher education as conducted by a class group as an experience required for progress toward a baccalaureate degree. Current practice may be marred by bad attitudes, poor preparation, and misunderstanding; however, it is not the intention of the model to judge the quality of a particular mode of instruction.

How else could one go about analyzing the learning situation? The matrix technique lays out a grid against which current practice can be grouped and classified. It is primarily diagnostic and explorative. One alternative is direct experimentation, studying in a systematic way what happens when a specific element in the learning experience is varied. In small and scattered ways this has been done; however, these segments do not represent a continuous coverage and many are just impressions, not quantitative data. Another limitation of direct experimentation is the reluctance of teachers to subject college students to the total gamut of the experimental range.

A second alternative to model-building is simulation. This could be as complex as a computer game played by the people normally involved in the learning situation, or it could be role-playing. It would be possible to place the variables of the learning experience in a mathematical expression and to try different parameters. For example, the length of the class period is usually held constant, and this parameter of an hour's length appears frequently. Experience could be drawn from the schools using ninety-minute periods or from those with no fixed length. Another parameter is the average levels of achievement as measured by grades. With pass/fail some interesting alternatives are being explored. To do either of these by simulation is difficult, and most are content to imagine what might happen. The use of the computer to create a dialogue between the student and the faculty member replicated the tutorial system but with many more possibilities. We have several years experience using the computer to simulate the teacher. Efforts are now being made by General Electric Company and others to simulate the student's responses.

If among the alternatives, a matrix is used to analyze collegiate learning it might be well to throw out some philosophical conjecture. Does the impact of technologies expressed in media and space arrangements make radical or just small differences in the learning outcomes? Are students really interested in how they learn and therefore in the exploration of very different learning situations? To what extent will students tolerate experimentation, taking the risk that goes with it? Is the current concern about teaching a real expression of dissent about the teaching or the muscle flexing of a lifelong urge to be one's own master and to participate early in what he becomes? Will the faculty embrace change if they see meaningful alternatives, or are the weight of tradition and the vested interest and advantages already won more attractive? Is the federal government likely to be the agency that sees the need for using other parts of the learning experience continuum? And lastly, using McLuhan's concepts of hot and cold media, is too much hot or saturated media such as a lecture now in use?

One of the incentives to build a model is the feeling that many people have become concerned about higher education and that much thinking in industry and business is directed toward alternative techniques. The frenetic pace at trade conferences such as the Department of Audio Visual Instruction makes this evident. The electronic world holds much promise. It is willing to take on the teacher as it did the housewife half a century ago, promising to make the teacher's lot much easier and pleasant. Its most fearsome concomitant is the hazard in this complex operation of making the teacher remote, limited to operating a console or keeping him preoccupied with more incoming data than he can easily handle. But there have always been the Cassandras and those who are afraid to open Pandora's box.

The development of group dynamics as a technique has opened up the inner world of the classroom and by it, access to powerful emotional forces. These are not now very well controlled and are likely to be misunderstood, manipulated, and misused before fuller understanding is developed. Sensitivity training sessions may be bitter experiences for some although the group as a whole may profit from their use. The electronic and the emotional levers can be used to widen the gap between the most and least able student instead of being used to help the group to help one another. Certainly space configurations through new concepts and architecture provide greater flexibility. There is no longer need for windows. Conveying education to where the student is, makes his learning carrel the library or even his residence. Withdrawal of the university from the pastoral sanctuary with walls to a place that maximizes the learning opportunity will remove the whole concept of *in loco parentis*. It will be a bona fide part of the community, and the student will not feel the transition when he completes the formal phase of his educational training and enters the working world.

the complement of persons

The parameters of learning are contained in the seven categories of the model or matrix. The matrix becomes a taxonomy or a handy means of describing different learning situations and classifying them. The first category or axis has for its subject the people involved in the learning situation. The human involvement in the learning situation is best described when several subscales are used. For example, it requires information about the number of participants, both teachers and students. This might be called the mix.

In addition to the number of people there are subtle distinctions such as the role played and the gap between senior (teacher) and junior learners. At mid-scale the ratio of one teacher to twenty learners is a parameter. It is interesting to explore the extremes of this scale contemplating how a million students could profit from one teacher or, at the opposite end, how one hundred teachers could assist one student. At still a different point on the scale would be ten teachers meeting with ten students.

Often the gap between the senior and junior learners is

small, such as the case of a graduate student teaching a
freshman class. Occasionally a person as great as a Nobel
Prize winner may teach freshman chemistry. Subscales can
be helpful in identifying such relationships as student
teacher gaps, role changes of the participants and primary
versus secondary involvement. The people dimension has
been selected as the first category because of its centrality
to the learning experience. The human input is an essential and constant relationship during the period of the
learning situation.

the space configuration

The space involved in the learning situation is the second
essential dimension. Space may be considered at three levels. There is outer space. This is the surrounding space to
the classroom or learning area. It begins with the campus
and moves outward to the world at work or at war. The exterior connections occur through noise, signals, and contemporary data. The second level is the classroom itself.
This immediate environment contained within the capsule
or class envelope, describes the majority of activities toward which attention is focused. Not all classes are held in
a fixed environment, and within the classroom itself significant variations in interaction can be made. The third level
is the inner dimension of the feelings and interpersonal reactions of the participants. Thus openness or alienation,
competitiveness or cooperativeness, isolation or fraternity
describe important characteristics of the space relationships in the learning situation.

Today it is possible to think of a class learning situation
in which the participants are dispersed; the class does not

meet at one place at one time. One may then ask why is it a class? If it presumes a common learning experience with relative, fixed relationships between the individuals, the space in which it occurs may not be too significant. For example, a class may go on a field study or on a library search and not be together except at the planning and evaluation stages. It is also possible for class members to do most of their work outside the class keeping in contact with each other and the instructor by telephone or a message handling system. The several segments of the space category may overlap, and the perimeter of the class envelope may expand or contract markedly.

the process involved

The third dimension of the matrix is the process involved. It follows after people and space categories as the most significant part of the experience. It represents an overall description of what is happening in the class and defines the mode of learning. Common terms associated with mode are lecture, discussion, laboratory, and evaluation. A new set of definitions needs to be found to place these time-honored modes in a more systematic format. The remaining four categories are closely related to the overall process; input, output, interaction, and the time. Until these terms are defined, it may appear that more than one process is used at a given time or in sequence within the hour, but this overlap is mainly a matter of definition.

The classroom activity or process is usually designated by a broad term meaning different things to different people and expressed differently depending upon the teacher. Not all of the activity in the classroom is initiated by the teacher. In one way or another any activity in the classroom contributes to or detracts from the learning process. The intentional methods are usually clearly understood and frequently used. Lecturing or presenting material and ideas heads the list followed by recitation, discussion, problem solving, and testing. Not all classroom behavior is verbal or written. Many activities are symbolic and require cues such as the raised hand, the look in the eye, the use of visuals and even touch.

the time relationship

The fourth category is time. This dimension until recently wasn't a likely dimension, but today it is possible by preprogramming and rerunnning of tapes to place within the classroom period canned materials and to use them in a mixed time relationship. Thus we now can talk about real time and nonreal time and then intermix them. The pre, real, post, and lapsed times are of interest because of the flexibility they provide to participants. It is also possible to place groups of materials before a student simultaneously requiring reception of two inputs at once. The effect of all this "time-bending" is to make it possible that the student can receive information when convenient. It also creates the hazard of letting the teacher control time by forcing the student to accept materials at a rate not of his own choosing.

Another asset of time flexibility is that it can extend a learning time for the participants. A lecture can be heard again by a tape reproduction. A student can prepare beforehand as readily as the teacher. The student can also review later. It makes it possible for the student to use video tape playback for an instant repeat or a review at a much later time. Some aspects of time flexibility occur with library books because a book is one of the oldest stored data text sources in a cumbersome subworkable retrieval system. The notes of the student arc another form of information available at the time and choosing of the student. Recent studies of speech compression, time-lapse photography, and holography open additional opportunities for time flexibility for both students and the teacher.

inputs to the learning situation

As a fifth category, the inputs to the learning situation become a dimension along which the resources and materials can be stretched out and grouped in subcategories. One first thinks of formal materials, such as lecture materials, problems, and projects as inputs; however, each person brings to the class a number of skills and attitudes that are actively used in the learning situation. Thus the formal and informal inputs must be considered. Often a pretest is used to determine the knowledge of the class about a subject at the time of entry into the courses. Most of these instruments measure only a small part of the resources that are set in motion as the class begins. It is still very difficult to determine the starting point in a learning situation. Although we may not for some time be able to measure completely all the inputs, it is possible now to examine in a systematic fashion the various kinds of inputs in the hope that they will be matched up later with outputs so that an objective measure of class progress may be obtained. For the purposes of this study the subscales or the category of inputs will include such things as knowledge, skills, past experience, and attitudes.

interaction in the learning setting

A sixth category, and one of unusual interest, has to do with the techniques of feedback sometimes called transference. This is the means by which the people in the learning situation interact and exchange ideas. On the assumption that a learning situation is never a completely one-way transmission, the people in it become junior and senior learners and each profits in some way from the experience. In formal learning experiences such as the lecture there may be interruption for questions or discussion. There are the more subtle responses such as inattention, laughter, handraising, and other signaling devices by which the teacher-actor, plying his art, senses the reaction to what he does. One subscale under feedback would be the classification of the kinds of responses used.

On the assumption that a class makes progress towards its intended goal, e.g. increased knowledge in a subject field, a number of techniques have been developed to enhance class progress by feedback between its members. This two-way transmission occurs before and after class as well as in the class. Students share information about their progress on assignments and make comments about what has happened in class. Teachers meet in conference with students and often talk about their attitudes toward the course. Occasionally there is sufficient openness in the class for the group to discuss their interpersonal relationships. The nature of the feedback changes with the size and advanced standing of the class. In a large lecture individual response is minimized, and total class response such as a groan, a cheer, or general inattention may be the only means. By contrast, a seminar is arranged so that members of the group attain peer status in that each presents his paper to the class and receives the comments from others. The purpose of the seminar is for mutual help as well as general learning for all.

The techniques for feedback or transference are endless and often subtle. The important signals given by eye, hand, or posture have been informally recognized by generations of teachers. The use of recitation, problem solving, and subgroup discussion groups provide enriched opportunities for feedback. New techniques such as telephone call back to television programming as in the University of Florida program called Genesys demonstrate that physical remoteness can be overcome and that responses can be made at the same time a lecture is in progress.

Of particular interest in an educational world, now saturated with media information, is the need to develop techniques by which two or three inputs can be filtered and reacted to. In the simple illustration of listening to a television program students may converse while watching the program so that two levels of communication are occurring simultaneously or in rapid sequence. The television newscaster with the bug in the ear gathers additional data even as he reports what he knows. The television crew members are linked together by throat mikes and single earphones so that they may carry on a running conversation and yet attend to the televised action at close range. These concepts could be extended to three-level interactions. If the rate of change continues to accelerate, and man becomes saturated with media from both printed and electronic means, the person in the classroom or in the world must develop the discipline of discriminate sensation reception or be prepared to cope with the frustration of simultaneous transmissions. Thoughtful educators and psychologists have already gathered data to document these tensions. To what extent man will accommodate to his enriched environment or withdraw from it is of more than passing interest. The purpose of Chapter 7 on feedback in this book is to outline in a systematic way how the classroom situation is a part of this broad range of feedbacks and transference.

the outputs of the learning situation

The seventh and last category is titled the consequence of the learning experience. In terms of functional management theory, and increasingly that of education, this consequence is referred to as an output. Much attention has been focused upon output often measured by grades, degrees, scholarships, and the permission to go on for advanced-level work. A continuing problem with this aspect of the learning experience has been the inability to measure in a quantitative fashion what has happened. If some gross measure of what has happened can be determined, it is still difficult to separate it from what the learner had already acquired at the beginning of the class experience. If there is hope that higher education will measure achievement not by the time served in class, or the number of courses taken, but by proficiency measured in terms of output, a new era will have been ushered in. Grades may become a measure not only of achievement but of progress.

It is the purpose of the chapter on outputs to look at the present status of the use of output information and to provide a number of subscales on which further information might be collected.

Among the scales that must be considered are those which deal with attitudinal change on the part of the learner as well as factual knowledge. The dependence on the ability to repeat back in either written or oral form is but one measure of output. Another scale would be the kind of behaviorial change that actually takes place as a result of the learning experience. This may be necessarily latent as in the teacher, engineer, or doctor, and the effect of a course in literature or music appreciation may not be measurable directly or immediately. There is also the scale of a person's progress compared to others in the class and the relative value of one kind of achievement compared to another. It is possible that one will look at outputs in terms of the lattice of a student's accomplishments and look to the class to enable the student to build his complete mastery of the field as an individual pattern which would still fit the needs of the class as a whole. It would then be interesting to relate these accomplishments to his known characteristics socially and intellectually. It comes close to what David Riesman discovered that some colleges produce in students, a style of life.

These seven categories—People, Space, Process, Time, Inputs, Interactions, and Outputs—become the categories covering the whole spectrum of the class learning experience in higher education, and each category has a series of subscales along which particular classroom experiences can be arranged. Each category will be explored more fully looking to the parameters each experience contains. It will be of interest to explore the portions of the grid that are seldom used. Is this paucity due to lack of equipment for implementation, anticipated inefficiency, or just the lack of pioneers? What is being done with the extremes of the continuum? Should serious consideration be given to a class of a million students listening to one teacher? Should there ever be a class of one student taught by one hundred teachers? There was such a case when Col. Frank Borman was briefed by a panel of experts in 1966 before his long space flight. A two-day session was devoted to the interpersonal and physical problems of a ten-day voyage costing 350 million dollars. Other fringes of the grid need investigation, such as multiple feedback and individualized approaches in a class environment.

Not until recently have the flexibilities of the concept of continuous progress in higher education been explored. This eliminates the start-stop punctuation of the twelve-week course and the fifty-minute period. The concept of the university without a campus is still rather fresh as is the redeployment of resources by interinstitutional media networks. As television took its place in modern society within one generation, the commitment of much lecture material to video and audio tape could also occur in one generation with only occasional updating. If the option is taken to use this, will it lead to an industrial-type production slant seeking efficiencies and innovations to gain competitive advantage? The flexibilities at hand provide multiple options to institutions of higher education, and major decisions must be made.

One task, using the grid as a matrix of total possibilities, is to find the places where technology is ahead of practice and also to find places where practice is ahead of technology. Lecture consoles can now be devised which provide more data feedback than a lecturer can assimilate and immediately use to redirect his lecture. Thus man can no longer keep up with the rate with which his technology can operate. By contrast many who teach are reluctant to commit in full confidence all their class procedures to technical devices. Few are failproof, and there is seldom a suitable backup if the original plan goes awry. Although reliability has increased, one either opts for the occasional malfunction or becomes a tinkerer of sorts to rescue situations.

As an example of the grid applied to three quite different modes of class instruction, figure *1* shows a lecture with three hundred students, a discussion with thirty students, and a student response system with eighty students. The typical procedure used for each of the seven dimensions of the learning experience is given for the three kinds of groups.

1. Procedures Used in Three Types of Classroom Situations

	Large Lecture	Discussion	Student Response
People	1/300	1/30	1/80
Space	Lecture Hall	Seminar Room	Classroom
Process	Lecture	Discussion Recitation	Discussion Poll taking
Time	Mixed modes	Real time	Real time(on-line)
Inputs	Pretest	Individual interrogation	Inventory class knowledge
Interactions	Prof to Students	Prof to Students Students to Prof	Prof to Students Students to Prof Students to Students
Outputs	Final Exam	Accumulation quizzes and recitations	Frequent probes by computer printout

In summary, an analysis of classroom practices on a two-dimensional grid is but a device to aid the thinking of those who plan for the future. New techniques have arrived pell-mell. Some sorting and sifting is needed if a broad and meaningful approach is to be made to the challenges facing higher education.

parameter 1

the
complement of persons

OF the seven descriptive categories of the collegiate learning experience, the first describes the people involved. The learning situation implies a learning group. This includes the active participants and also those who are indirectly involved such as media teams and planners.

The primacy of this category in the matrix stems from the fact that it is difficult to conceive of a learning situation without people. Cartoonists have fun depicting a classroom situation in which the teacher is replaced by a tape recorder and the students in response have replaced themselves with tape recorders at each seat. This does not subtract people from the learning situation. It only illustrates the flexibilities of preprogramming and postlistening. The outcomes of the learning experience must affect people, and the inputs must be the works of people either live or prerecorded. The task of preparation requires the effort of live people. The computer which some think will replace thinking has been aptly described as fast, accurate, and stupid. Although it is possible to store the combined efforts of millions of people, it in no way replaces the original efforts of these persons. Junior and senior learners are the indispensable agents in the learning process. A number of subscales are useful to describe the variety of ways people can be grouped and caused to interact in the learning situation. Among these are the size of the group, its mix and hierarchy of experience, the roles participants play, and the personal relationships between individuals.

subscales:
size, mix, and role of learners

With respect to size, the learning group can be as small as two persons or as large as technology will permit. It could be two students learning together or a single student in communication with stored responses in a learning device. Today we can conceive of a group as large as a million listeners to a single teacher.

Consideration of size brings one to the consideration of the hierarchy within the class or the mix of teachers and students. Assuming that some in the class act as senior learners and provide the impetus for the learning of others (usually called students), there are the identifying characteristics of mix and gap. By mix is meant the ratio of teachers to students. Assuming at the outset that all are learning in a teaching situation, some in the group take on the task of leading the others. In team teaching this may be several persons. Frequently it is only one. In occasional cases it can be a great many teachers.

The other part of the subscale describing mix is the gap between the teacher and the student. In typical college learning situations a sizable gap either real or imagined exists between the teacher and the group of students. Occasionally, however, a graduate student is used and his status and competence affect the relationship between himself and the class. The gap is lessened. The gap is eliminated completely in a graduate seminar in which all persons participate equally with little differentiation of level. There is still another facet to the matter of gap as it applies to the student group. Although there are efficiencies to be gained by grouping people for the learning process, individual differences exist, and there is the tension between the best speed for the individual and that for the group.

Another subscale describes the role played by the participants. Because of the complexity of human relationships, an individual does not remain always active or passive, self-seeking or group oriented, but changes his style from time to time. The teacher may pause for recitation or even take on a listening role while a student makes a class report. People do take on varied roles in the learning situation, and the subscale simply takes account of it.

These relationships of people in the learning situation when looked at systematically by the subscales show surprising patterns. Graduate teaching assistants find themselves at times less knowledgeable than some of the more able students in their classes. At a seminar the individual who is presenting his ideas may not have as large a grasp of the subject as the collective wisdom of his peers. Able students may suppress much that they know to gain social acceptance in a class. Better understanding of human relationships and the willingness to venture toward conditions of trust have led some teachers to experiment with great openness in class inviting criticism and personal feeling. Most surprising of all is the great willingness of students to teach themselves and each other. This has always occurred informally but now is viewed as a useful part of the formal process. Free schools and other efforts to control their own learning show that students are willing to try many peer-oriented variants.

These subscales help define the characteristics of the people in the learning situation. Among these scales certain points will be found where much of current practice now accumulates. The ratio of students to teachers in a classroom is most frequently about twenty to one. The most frequent mix is one teacher to a class of students. This parameter has not varied much although there are now more examples of large classes and team teachers. Between the senior and junior-level learner the gap is now diminishing because fewer faculty have advanced degrees, and more teaching is done by graduate assistants. The rapid rise of the community college adds to the closure of this gap. Actually there has developed a third party relationship. The gap is not so much between the two participants in the learning process as it is with an increasing body of materials both must know. This storage of knowledge and skills had been accumulating quietly but impressively in texts and library books but now also in a growing variety of media devices. No one completely masters today's knowledge. The student seeks the source that will give him most help. This may not always be the teacher when standardized tests or specific competencies are the goal.

Beyond the subscales already mentioned is yet another characteristic of a learning group, namely its overall purpose. For what reason did the group get together? It may be voluntary. It may seek credit toward a degree, or there may be other reasons. There may be the expectation of repeated meetings with accumulation of effort. The group may develop a sense of trust or openness or act only as a collection of individuals. Each of these factors makes a difference in the way the skills of the teacher are employed in leading a class. A class may be heterogeneous expecting different things from the same teacher. The right amount of permissiveness, directiveness, and individual help is hard to fit to a class. Compromises are struck, and working arrangements are made that become a background for the primary task of learning.

levels of learner involvement

There are three concentric circles of involvement of the persons in the learning situation. The outer ring relates the learning group to the world beyond the classroom which has ringing telephones, next appointments, and possibly a student riot. There is the middle circle of the class itself; usually enclosed in a room and shut away from the exterior world physically. The group may limit itself to this space envelope or go beyond the immediate environment by field trips, media connections, or by not limiting the experience to the classroom from the start.

There is a third or inner ring of each person's attitudes and attachments brought in from the past or developed during the class. Certainly many romances begin in college through classroom associations. Learning carrels are now planned for two or more participants. When discussion or small-group projects are made a part of the class, members find the interpersonal relationships important to the learning situation. These three concentric rings or spheres of influence are still another subscale of the "people involved" category. Its parameter is all too often the middle ring.

Much of the concern about teaching has bypassed these three levels of involvement. The insularity of teaching in

what is often called irrelevance may be traced to the cocoon of classroom group isolation. Not all lock the door of
the classroom and turn the world off. More than ever the
outer world is connected to the classroom by a semipermeable membrane. By media, work-study plans, and the more
informal setting of many classes, contemporary experience
becomes a part of the class concern. By dress and other arti-
facts students signal back their reaction to the world about
them. Often experts are brought to class, and occasionally
open admission for any curious person is allowed. More
and more classes find exotic settings which link them with
the outer world. Chapman College uses an ocean liner to
give students a firsthand acquaintanceship with Europe
and Asia. Many universities have campuses overseas. Life
science departments require experience at experimental
stations, and fledgling teachers do supervised teaching
while living in the community where their pupils live. The
interaction with people beyond the classroom by conference telephone calls, television, and the aforementioned
means make the classroom truly a university without walls.

Although it might be presumed from the foregoing that
the class is enduring as an entity, no assurance can be given
that we will learn in class-sized clusters in the future. The
persistance of this pattern is remakable, and it is comfort-
ing to think that it will continue for some time. This may
be simply the basic desire of people to be with other people
while learning. The elements of competition, contrast, and
mutual help are all there. On the other hand, students
learn at different rates, and the class unless small, or creatively taught, tends to move forward in lockstep. The class
also has an unfortunate ratio of leadership to followership.
It may be financially expedient but as far as maximum
learning is concerned, few students are being used to their

maximum capacity. This is one reason why the work of the professor placed in an efficient dispensing device, such as a computer, may seem to the individual student to be more responsive in the total number of exchanges in an hour than the student experienced in the usual classroom situation.

Let us look for a moment at the kind and level of participants. The titles given to teacher and student are time-honored but need closer inspection. Perhaps it should be required that each teacher learn something from his pupils and vice versa. A relationship not entirely wholesome develops between senior and junior learners when the authoritative grading technique and credit-earning requirements are imposed. In the British system where the lecture has been disassociated from the examination, the strength lies in the student's freedom to be a member of the class or not as he wishes. The weakness lies in the professor's proclivity to teach whatever he feels is of interest, without direct regard for the examination itself. This thrusts upon the tutor the role of intermediary. In the American model the teacher is in a position to excite his students, but too often trades upon the helplessness of his captive audience. In situations where students grade each other, or where the course is defined in such a way that for specific attainments a given grade may be had, the role played in the class frequently changes. Students endeavor to complete work at the earliest time possible, and a large number of them select the requirements for the grade of their choice. More study is needed to gain understanding of these roles in terms of the techniques employed.

Within the middle sphere of the class environment, the part played by a particular participant will change by self-initiation or by the teaching techniques employed. For example, the teaching technique of subgroup discussion involves many more people in an active role. The teacher may become the dispenser of new information or a gadfly in a matter of strongly held opinions. With respect to self-initiation some may fall asleep or drop out. The number of participants (full time equivalent) may vary widely as individuals opt in or out. Later as interactions are discussed (Chapter 9), procedures to estimate the human involvement will be described. It seems reasonable to suppose that, in any group process involving individuals of varying ability, the completion rates on any topic or problem will be different, and some accommodation for this idle time in changed roles is to be expected. This is only to intimate that role development in college-level groups is highly complex. It may be beyond any quantitative analysis for some time. Observations of this behavior and broad descriptive terms will be of value now in improving the learning situation itself.

The third circle is the inner world of the people in the class. Students who have come together to learn, unless the class is very large, usually find some interrelationships that are meaningful. If competition for a limited number of A's does not ruin rapport, the members of the class may develop a level of openness or trust by which they are able to help each other and find easier acceptance of their own ideas. Such a group can become goal-oriented and progress towards its goals at a more efficient pace. Few teachers allow this degree of flexibility and depend upon maintaining a differential between themselves and the class so that an authoritative stance can be maintained. At times there are breakthroughs in any class, such as the flashes of humor, insight, and interest in others.

Another dimension to the inner world of people is the

rate of progress that is possible with people who learn via speech, visuals, and other techniques. Speech is a slow media compared to our reading comprehension. A teacher can speak no more than two hundred words a minute while the mind may comprehend three times that much. It allows time for daydreaming, idea formation, and reflective pauses for insight. Unfortunately too often it is used for note-scribbling, and wondering which part of what is being spoken will have to be repeated on a test. The persistence of the lecture with its spoken mode of operation does have a great virtue. It is an accommodation to the average rate at which a group can progress.

No exploration of the inner world of people in a class would be complete without consideration of the diversion from the subject at hand that is supported at times by both teacher and students. This can be planned or, as it most often happens, is unplanned. It is natural for a group to encourage convergent thinking because common interests and goals usually draw a group together. Creativity flourishes best in an atmosphere of divergence, and the group's ability to accommodate to these excursions is a measure of its maturity. Most of the time these diversions are quietly individual, occurring nonverbally in the mind. One can skip ahead of the trend of discussion to form ideas, questions, puns or concepts not directly related to the class. There is the hazard of inattention, and one must learn the art of coming back to the subject at hand. Not enough is yet known about how groups learn to decide that laminar flow of ideas, like traffic, moves a group further ahead in a given time.

Any learning group must set up its fences against the introduction of extraneous matters or at least determine the limits it will tolerate. In a complex and pluralistic so-

ciety few learning groups can remain narrowly in pursuit
of a specific subject field. Many interactions take place in
class other than those directly related to the course material. Give a class a five-minute break and observe the matters discussed in the hallways. With college groups the hidden agenda includes sex, sports, drugs, and a variety of
philosophical issues. Friendships develop setting up paired
relationships or in-groups. This quiet struggle to direct the
activities of the group will not go away if ignored. It becomes a significant part of the people-dimension in the
learning situation.

people and technology in perspective

What is the impact of technology on the people involved in
the learning situation? Most important is the flexibility of
scale. A million people can hear and see one teacher. A
hundred experts can be drawn together by conference
phone for consultation with one person such as the president of a nation or a brain surgeon. Will these economies
of scale be looked upon as a means of reduced costs of
higher education or as a means of finding funds to enrich
other parts of education where one-to-one ratios are more
effective? Most important to the future of the teaching profession is its own primacy in this task. The feasibility of
large-scale presentations is likely to create a small corps of
nationally syndicated lecture-performers and a larger
group of less visible teachers. More time will be spent in
preparing materials than in presenting them. The potential for using people more effectively is greater with technology. So is the potential for abuse of people.
   From the student's side of the desk the resources avail-

able to the student increase mightily. Libraries are the classic example of a resource greater than the combined wisdom of the faculty. If most of what any professor has to offer is on tape and available at any time, the library has been greatly expanded. All that is lacking is the opportunity for immediate interaction, and even that can be helped by technology.

People will find closer and more varied relationships in the learning experience or at least the potential for these closer relationships will exist. The interconnections among the three spheres of people relationships are now better understood, and equipment exists to implement many of these relationships. The chart of subscales, figure *2,* gives

2. Relationships of People Involved in Learning Situations

Distribution Scale	Estimates[1]				
	Enrichment Extreme	Upper Quartile	Average Practice	Lower Quartile	Efficiency Extreme
	2%	25%	50%	25%	2%
1. *Size of Student Group*	1	10	20	100	One million
2. *Mix Teacher/Student*	10/1	1/10	1/20(2/40)	1/100	Team/1,000,000
3. *Gap Teacher/Student Ability*	1/1	2/1	4/1	10/1	Varied
4. *Role Students active/passive*	2/1	1/2	1/10	1/100	1/1,000,000 plus whispering
5. *Spheres Involved*					
% Outer (World)		33	5	0	
% Middle (Class)	Varies	33	90	100	Varies
% Inner (Selfs)		33	5	0	
6. *Personal Relationships*[2] *trust/adversary*	10/1	1/1	1/10	1/100	most fellow students not seen

[1] Based on observations and opinions of experts
[2] Assumes a grading system

estimates of present practice as a central parameter and the directions in which practice is enriched or made more efficient. Its purpose is to illustrate the subscales and general trends.

parameter **2**

the
space configuration

EVERY learning situation in higher education has a space
envelope. This space configuration is the area defined by
the environment in which the participants carry out their
activities. Historically this has been the schoolhouse. Its
borders are as broad as the campus or as narrow as the log
on which Mark Hopkins and a student sat. Space is important and its significance is complex and subtle. Just as
there are outer and inner ranges of people involvement
in the previous category, so there are peripheral as well as
intimate environments. A campus, or even a total city, can
be relevant to the learning of a group. At the same time
the rapport between two classmates who meet at a coffee
house may be a great stimulus to learning. This dimension
of space is readily defined in quantitative terms and represents a very wide variety of environments.

The dimension of space in higher education has for its
parameter the classroom. This constant has for centuries
defined the campus yet it is but one part of a cluster of

enclosures such as the library and refectory that make up the academic space configuration. Figure 3 attempts a scheme of this interrelationship.

3. Space Configurations Related to Group Learning in Higher Education: Group Space and Other Space Used by Students

space relationships	macro-peripheral	group size immediate	mini-individual
	Public Multigroup	*Group*	*Subgroup*
Specific Kinds of Space	Campus Buildings Community World bookstores theatres bars concert halls sports arenas stores factories government buildings outdoor recreation	Lecture Halls Classrooms Seminar Rooms Laboratories Lounges Corridors Outdoor Gatherings Bus	Individual Library Carrels Living-learning Center Date Room Study Residence Hall Room Auto Tutorials Faculty Offices Special Labs (computed) Selfinstruction Labs Automobile Public Transportation Queues Homes
Linkages Between Spaces	Broadcast Media Work-Study Programs Conferences Group Tours	Response System Simulated Environment Planetarium Link Trainer Computer Research Projects Visitors	Retrieval Systems Telephone Books Schedules Media Group Transport

the classroom and its context

The 7 million students on 2200 campuses "go" to class in much the same way. This "going to class" is a major portion of what they do for a degree. Informal groups cluster to discuss assignments and for mutual help, but a physical presence in an assigned place is still the rule. The space is designed for concentrating attention on the subject at hand. Thus four walls, chairs, and the convenience of heat and light constitute the bare essentials. Many enclosures have little more than that plus a blackboard. Few even have charts and visuals. It is often surprising how many more illustrations of student work and subject materials are on display in lower-school classrooms than in those of universities. The classroom is not an isolation booth. The peripheral space is significant.

By peripheral space is meant the larger context in which the learning situation occurs. In most instances of group experience in higher education there is a campus environment beyond the classroom which impinges on the classroom. There is also the immediate time before and after the class in which students flow to and from the surrounding area. In the case of commuting students it is often a sizable portion of the student's life. Car pools and reading on public transportation become an expected part of the corporate act.

It is difficult today to think of space apart from its communication links. These connections are now sufficiently effective (or the participants have become so accustomed to them) that at least a partial reality is obtained by being directly involved with persons at a distance. Closed-circuit TV can mold people separated by distance into a functioning relationship. In the past, groups in classes across a hallway were separated by a closed door. Today the relationship of the class to the surrounding environment is more that of a semipermeable membrane through which much of the outside world filters in but only a limited amount of this inside world filters out.

To what extent does the external world affect the learning group? In part it is a matter of subject content. If it is a class in fashion, foods, or even economics, the immediate relationship can be established. In engineering and teacher training it is connected but more casually. In fields like philosophy and history the relationship is less obvious.

The immediate class environment reflects a much more flexible concept of a space envelope than previously. Recently architects have felt free to try new seating arrangements, new acoustical treatments, and a much wider range of media devices. Often the floor is carpeted and the seating mobile. There is awareness that lighting, ventilation, freedom to move about, and acoustics all affect the learning group. The concept of moving learners to a fixed space to hear teachers still persists. A few lecture halls have been devised in which a rotating stage makes it possible for the laboratory class demonstration to be prepared and then rotated into place for the next class. At the New York World's Fair, the daring idea of seating visitors in capsules and moving them to the exhibit or demonstration was not continued at the exposition in Montreal nor has it reached the campus. The idea of continuous learning, which would lead to a variable-length period and an end to the present kind of scheduling and seating, has not taken hold.

Perhaps the concept of an enclosure should be changed because it sounds so restrictive. Yet an enclosure, whether it be a learning carrel for an individual or a class, is designed for the purpose of allowing concentration on the task at hand and to strain out extraneous matters. Recent studies of ambiant noise levels suggests that more external interaction can be tolerated than was thought. One advantage of the isolation of the present classroom is the opportunity it affords to see what effect color, light, and seating arrangements have on the participants. The classroom may now be seen as a total environment in which the place to read, write, think, and participate is coordinated with the resources to do it efficiently and comfortably. The enclosure provides a general ambiance which students can now describe as pleasant or unpleasant. Classrooms seating forty or fifty students describe the bulk of what is done in higher education. There are situations, however, in which the learners are dispersed, and the perimeter of the enclosure is the campus, the city, or whatever general environment the learners might encompass. For purposes of analysis four elements may be considered to make up the space dimension: the enclosure, the arrangement of the group, the physical facilities, and the link with the outer world.

The enclosure itself has yielded to innovations in building techniques about as dramatically as the suburban residence. Mobility has required that trailer-type classrooms be provided at least temporarily, and the concern for the dynamics of learning has led to the shaping of the exterior to provide these flexibilities. There is some trend toward larger learning spaces and many larger institutions can now afford the luxury of lecture halls seating over a thousand and keep them occupied all day long. Natural lighting has become less important and, in some cases, groups of classes have been placed beneath a mall (University of Illinois, Chicago Campus). The intermix of classrooms with faculty offices and study lounges influences favorably the student use of space. More often than not the architects and actual users of the building are brought together to create a program for the building with flow charts and opportunity for the users and the planners to exchange ideas.

In the typical situation the administration of an institution of higher education planning a new building appoints a faculty committee to have a part in writing the program for the new building. This program committee is usually briefed by the architects and then given opportunity for one or more visits to campuses where buildings have been recently constructed. Without this look at current practice there is a temptation of a committee to replicate the structures of their alma maters or their favorite example of architecture on the campus. The acoustics, the textures, the colors, and the comfort, as well as the seating now command more attention. Attachments to the classroom are more frequent such as observation windows, adjacent laboratories, rear screen projection windows, and raceways beneath the floor for electronic cables. Occasionally only three of the four walls of a classroom are constructed, depending upon the lowered noise level by acoustical treatment for the more open arrangement. The classroom, however, is still the dominant type of enclosure constructed. A small but increasing fraction of space is built as self-instruction space or areas called study areas which in effect are enlarged hallways in which students can gather informally.

The class enclosure has too often been a tight little island. Today this enclosure may be a lounge area in the student's residence hall or even the study desk in his bedroom. When the connections to the student are made by closed-circuit television or preprogrammed material, it is more difficult to prescribe the dimensions of the space enclosure.

As additional evidence of the flexibility in making classrooms more dynamic, the position of the teacher has become unglued. In larger classrooms the podium still makes it hard for the teacher to roam freely about the class and multimedia tend to fix his location, however, this need not be so. Some classroom situations allow the student to come and go freely because the acoustical arrangements and the task of the class provide for this and others are not hindered in their work.

There is experimentation particularly in community colleges with enclosures involving more than one class and several teachers. Simultaneously many small groups may be meeting in the larger area. This larger envelope provides much the same flexibility as the enclosed mall shopping center. Light, heat, and sound are adjusted to make study activities for the individual, small groups, and even modest-size lecture groups. The total effect is to focus on the learner and to maximize his learning opportunity. This means that the teacher is no longer the focus of attention. The learning resources have become central. The teacher is the important programmer and the most important resource.

Perhaps out of necessity, but hopefully more out of purpose, the hourly movement of students with the accompanying hallway jams between classes is giving way to more off-hour and irregular scheduling. This accommodates small groups, individual interests, and the concept of continuous progress. The batch process which for so long directed learning into hour segments and the movements between enclosures to a ten-minute period shows signs of weakening. For one thing, the idea of continuous progress

in learning makes the environment available as long as the
student can profit from it and for as many successive days
as needed until a sufficient level of attainment has been
achieved. Placing the student more on his own in terms of
his discovery of ideas and using the peer group to assist in
the learning process breaks down the idea of fixed size and
length of classes. It is not entirely unexpected that the
community college would be first to develop this flexibility. It may have taken the cue from a number of campus-
style high schools. Relatively few of the four-year institutions have developed this amount of freedom.

The great variety of courses open to a college student
give a new kind of flexibility not open to the high school
or even the junior college student. With a greater variety
of teaching techniques and with a greater variety of
courses, tension mounts when the student is required to
take a prescribed program for which the courses have already been selected. This wide variety of courses and a
sufficient number of students must be placed in the boxes
called classrooms by a sizeable clerical force who labor
over the mechanics of teaching supply and class loads. In
larger schools the selection of a particular instructor by the
students has also been eliminated. This preoccupation
with filling boxes may forestall the serious consideration
needed for the total environment of a college freshman.
It would be preferable to have the student select the
teacher and the style of teaching he most enjoys and even
be free to select some irrelevant and inappropriate courses.
This would increase the student's sense of self-determination but would also give the faculty member the feeling
that he had a group of volunteers and not conscripts.

Today's classroom is furnished approximately as well as
the average home in a suburban community. It tends to

follow the other kinds of enclosures such as motels and jet planes where heavy traffic patterns are expected and a wide variety of uses are intended. More carpeting is evident. There is better lighting and more communication equipment. The elementary schools were the first to get this face-lifting because of the baby boom after World War II, and now that the enrollment bulge has pushed through higher education, new facilities on most campuses are comparable to the homes, churches, and public accommodations in the better neighborhoods. Since planning for these furnishings seems to be in the hands of architects and business oriented people, faculty interest has not always been fully met. Students have seldom been consulted, at least formally. However, they have been observed and their opinions reflected. Accommodating those who have sight or hearing deficiencies has only begun, although the handling of left-handed writers and extremes of height and weight have been well handled. The most dramatic improvements have occurred in lighting, acoustics, and comfortable seating.

Along with the luxury of modern classroom settings has come the need for proper maintenance. Classroom usage now approximates the behavior in the home and raises the question of smoking in the classrooms, of storage space for personal clothing and books, and the acoustical problem raised by people wanting to talk during formal presentations. The ability to regroup furniture in the classroom for different styles of instruction has yet to be perfected as does the way of dividing a large enclosure into smaller ones at modest cost with reasonable effort. New classrooms have provided for cable conduits to each seat to which wires may be run for later use of electronic equipment. This adds only a small amount to the cost but is frequently left out of final plans. A suitable stand or enclosure for projection equipment is only occasionally provided. This economy is more than counterbalanced by the cost of a staff of trained people to make these materials available when needed by the instructor and represents a division of labor within the teaching profession that has not yet been fully accepted.

An important decision in devising a building for classroom purposes involves the flexibility of classroom space. Partitions between classrooms may be made movable at considerable cost. Modular design may make it possible to move wall structures in reasonably short periods of time. Until recently the plastered wall was used because of its wide acceptance in the schools, but it proved to be difficult to modify without considerable cost and mess. Happily, architectural forms now provide wide-open spaces without supporting columns and modular outlets for light and climate control so that partitions can be erected wherever and whenever necessary. In practice few schools have made much use of this flexibility. In a check of several recently built buildings with modular utilities and movable walls, less than five percent of the structures had been moved in a two-year period. If partitions are easily movable, they are seldom satisfactory acoustically. This is not to say that architects are not arriving at a point at which the space envelope can be modified at modest cost and in short time. Access to these spaces has been made easier for students and faculty, and the pleasantness of the environment has certainly been improved.

beyond the traditional classroom

The links with the outer environment, and to some extent with the inner environment, of the students have been strengthened so greatly that it is now hard to tell where the classroom ends. Within the classroom the note taking, the memory, the daydreams have been mingled with the electronic connections to the outside world and sensitivity training for the inside world. By telephone, radio, television, newspapers, visitors, tape retrieval systems, and computers an almost bewildering array of sensory connections have been made to the world beyond. There is still the field trip and the laboratory, but even these have given way to the impact of technology. It is possible today to have a simulated environment as in a planetarium, a Link trainer, or the computer. The critical task is no longer finding ways to bring the resources of the world to the classroom but rather how to maximize their effectiveness and to prevent overstimulation and frustration. It is interesting that the window is disappearing from the classroom at the same time that media is pouring in.

Careful consideration is now being given in large universities to the impersonality of the learning situation. If truth is caught as well as taught, one wonders if the person who mediates it has effected an attitudinal impact on the student. The accumulation in a computer of the wisdom of many professors may not provide the individual feedback relationship that a student wishes. This link with the inner feelings of the student and the links of one student with another appear to be at the heart of the student concern for an adequate education. This concern is directed more at the faculty than at the administration, and it represents a deep concern and probably a valid one about the adequacy of the classroom procedures used for centuries for small groups of students and now multiplied by media for large numbers of students. This link with the teacher and the fellow student will be surrendered slowly if at all. The electronic and mechanical means of interconnection exist now in abundance. The problem is more the matter of managing this educational switchboard than it is thinking up a great many new ways to interconnect it.

How are people being related to spaces and educational circumstances today? Several years ago at the World's Fair in New York City many of the major exhibits brought people in groups to the media used to aid in the teaching process, such as the IBM people wall, the Vatican turntable, and the five people in an automobile drawn through an auto exhibit. Elevators, cars, escalators, and planes process people in a space envelope. The elementary schools have, on an experimental basis, taken groups of four about a table as a new module for learning. In learning carrels at high schools and universities, some are now planned for two, three, and four students. Because of tight time schedules and transportation difficulties, occasionally a scheduled classroom is dispersed, becoming available late at night or within one's own region, often as subgroupings. In many community colleges dual use of space has been provided by cafeterias becoming social halls, libraries, and classroom space. The language laboratory is both an individual teaching device but also a means for the teacher to listen in and, therefore, it serves a dual purpose. Space envelopes have become most flexible.

categories for space

Space as now being developed for classes in higher education is represented by at least three types. By far the most
common and oldest historically is the space enclosure for
thirty or forty students involving a single teacher, with or
without windows, nonvariable lighting, movable seating,
rectangular in shape with single-door entry. This represents the historic box which we have not yet outgrown. A
second type is planned for larger groups and is either pie-
shaped or oval with American or continental seating, some
provision for variable lighting and projection, occasionally
a rear screen. The lecturn provides instructor-control of
lighting and some audio and visual devices. Only occasionally is there a response system. The third type is represented by the self-learning situation in which carrels or
auto-tutorial laboratories are devised in the form of a
learning resources center. Often connected to the library
and with some professional assistance students self-schedule
themselves and operate in either a cafeteria or sequential
arrangement. This third type lends itself to decentraliza-
tion so that branches of these centers appear in residence
halls and within schools and departments of the university.

Recent concern about the increasing cost of higher education has led various states to require their public campuses to account for their use of space. Provision for additional space for added enrollment is based on square foot
estimates of what it takes to provide for students and
faculty members. Some differentiation for function has
already occurred. Space, then, has become a commodity
which has associated with it standard sizes for various functions and costs for given amounts. The accounting for the

use of space is still a gross measure and does not really pro-
mote innovations of efficiencies. In general, it can be said
that the doubling of enrollment in higher education has
been largely cared for with additional space. The new
space is more flexible and attractive than the old space.
Much of the old space is obsolete, but it continues to be
used and for some purposes, such as research and experimentation, is preferred to new enclosures. If all avenues of
improvement in higher education were to be examined,
one might rate very high the attractive external appearance
of buildings on recent campuses. Somewhat less high but
still among its most exciting adventures are the various
space envelopes for learning purposes planned in these
facilities.

What is the meaning of the great increase of space made
available to higher education? On the whole it has provided an attractive place for work and study and becomes
in itself a quiet revolution. Side by side with archaic buildings the new structures either tower upward or ramble
along the contour of the land in pleasing patterns. The
abrupt border between the exterior and interior of buildings is now softened by pedestrian malls and enclosed cor-
ridors. Gradually uniformity of architectural style has become secondary to the convenience of the enclosures. On
large campuses there is often a long distance to be traveled
between the academic complex, the residence hall, or the
parking lot. The few instances of integrated living and
learning have encountered mixed reactions. Apparently
there is no perfect solution to the configuration of enclosures a student or faculty member prefers in pursuit of his
concentrated effort and his diversified interests.

An important problem that space travelers are probing

in earnest, and those on earth must look to as well, is the concept of togetherness and isolation. Technology now gives us the potential to have people learn a large percentage of the accumulated knowledge of man in splendid isolation. This was true of libraries in the past, and the term bookworm may have been derived from it. If Leibnitz was the last living human to know all that was to be known at that time, the accumulation of knowledge today inundates man, and he must discover his own way to organize what he wants to include. At the college level this is often proscribed by the faculty, but there is still some discretionary time remaining. Patterns of association other than the required class capture the interest of students. Bull sessions become rappings. The group of students in the student union and the residence hall now spill over to the carpeted steps of educational buildings and the study nooks provided in many modern buildings. Although libraries have been reluctant to loan books for such natural study places, the dial-in tape retrieval device does make information available with little chance of loss.

Students are finding new patterns in which they like to learn. Most frequently this is in an informal space and with a relatively small group. They want to use their own natural leaders and occasionally want help from the faculty but on both a tell-me-like-it-really-is basis as well as I-want-to-answer-back basis. This new pattern may change the lecture style of the current classroom to the forum style of open discussion. When it is difficult to predict change more than a decade ahead in higher education and space envelopes are built for more than five decades, it gives one pause to think what the weight of tradition may do to later flexibilities. There is no question that space for this dialogue in higher education must be provided, but the means whereby the culture of a previous generation is passed on to the next may be far more by simulation in or out of a classroom than by the replication of textbooks through the vocal cords of an instructor in a classroom.

parameter **3**

the
process involved

definition of process

THE principal activity by which the hour's learning experience can be characterized best is called the process. Typical modes of the process are lecture, discussion, tutorial, seminar, and laboratory. Although several modes may be used in an hour, one mode usually dominates. The use of sequential and mixed modes needs to be recognized. During the major time intervals of the class period what persons do toward a common goal as a conscious part of the group is summed up in a general term which is a characteristic of the procedure.

In the case of a lecture one must consider what the other members of the group are doing, presumably listening. In a discussion there are the two sides of a dialogue—at least. During an hour period, a teacher may lecture, listen, conduct a drill, quiz a student, work a problem at the blackboard, and give sympathy to a troubled student. The students at the same time become listeners, participants, test takers, and occasionally daydreamers. Few hour sessions are purely one form, thus it is necessary to give a name to the general behavior of a group of people for moderate intervals of time.

For many years what went on in the classroom changed very little. The authority of the teacher remained unquestioned, discovery was subordinated to conformity, convergence of thinking was preferred to divergence, and the transmission possibilities were limited and in one direction only. Much of this is now undergoing a refreshing change, and a classroom partnership has evolved enlarging the variety of processes and changing the amount of usage of long established modes.

Just as there is an established complement of persons for a particular learning group and a defined space for meeting, there is a specific mode of operation which for a particular time can be described as the process. The total array of processes in use or imagined becomes a task for classification and interpretation.

classification of the process

Historically the names for the process have taken on topical references. This has been a way of telling the people what kind of activity to expect. Lectures are for listening, recitations are for telling back, and labs are for working experiments. By slight rearrangement this list of titles can be placed on a chart to show their affinity to the people and to some extent the space in the class. Figure *4* depicts this functional relationship.

The process can also be classified by its attributes. The list is endless. Is it old or recent? What does it cost? What

4. Relationship of Process to the People and Space of the Class

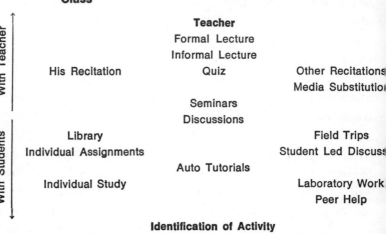

skills are needed? What kind of student can profit from it? What preparation time does it take? And there are the cross-relationships with other dimensions of the learning matrix: How large a group can be accommodated, what space is needed, can it be preprogrammed and what equipment is required.

For a given kind of process a cluster of attributes can be designated and defined. These clusters will overlap because the process is a gross rather than a precise entity at the start.

Actually more than 90 percent of current practice in the classroom can be described by less than a dozen title designations. The refinement of several terms such as discussion and laboratory require a frame of reference and further details about procedure.

Still other variables relate to the process. The frequency

of use, the appropriateness to the intended outcome, and the attitudes engendered in the participants are all significant. The list of processes is itself a taxonomy and calls for a judgment from the observer as to the appropriateness of the activity to the educational objective.

If a class is considered a group of learners, then a major responsibility is to see that these learners are efficiently handled. If it is assumed that this learning can be guided most efficiently by a single individual, the teacher, then he may choose the means by which he most often talks to the group. This systematic giving of information is generally called a lecture. If the faculty member allows little interruption, it might be called a formal lecture, but if he will allow students to raise questions or make comments it might be called an informal lecture. Not a very long step from the lecture is the discussion. The precise direction it will take is not known in advance; however, there is a goal in mind for which a general strategy is planned. The seminar is a special case of the discussion procedure in which the difference is primarily in the kind of learners. More mature learners gather to listen to one of their number make a report of his findings. After his report they raise questions and make a critical review of the substance of the report.

Moving farther from the teacher-directed process we come to the laboratory and the tutorial which provide a greater latitude for students to go at their own pace and to check back with the teacher only when necessary. This leads in turn to the other end of the scale at which the library and more recently the self-instruction centers are found. These help the student get as much of the material in a given subject field as he can on his own.

leaders and followers

The dimensions of the teaching process are seen too as the process in relationship to leadership in the learning situation. On the one extreme is the teacher-dominated situation with control of attention and task and at the other end the student-directed learning experience with the availability of the library and an array of packaged learning experience. Since forward progress in the learning process is anticipated, there is no meaningful alternative to the leadership function whether it comes from the senior partner or the peer group or both.

In practice the process is a complex matter which involves a leadership component, a followership readiness, a transmission device, a media, and a certain tempo. Perhaps the mystique of teaching is related to the blend of these elements into a style that best suits the teacher's handling of a group. It is also interesting to note that this style then impinges upon the process and casts the teacher as the stage director for the activity.

discovery and dissent

Assuming there is a flow of information and concept formation in a class, the reasons why this happens must be related to a need on the part of learners and the availability of a resource. The process depends upon a transmission device that is related first to the degree of freedom of the individuals involved and secondly to a least common path for the group. With respect to the first, although a good deal of freedom prevails, there is coercion in terms of obtaining credit, pleasing an instructor, obtaining a grade or being a contributing member of the peer group. With respect to the second, most classes fall into a pattern that best fits the needs of each. A teacher wanting recognition may find in lecturing the surest way to retain his leadership role. A student on the other hand, also seeking a place of leadership, may find that disrupting that class is his best way for recognition. If learning does take place some rapprochement is arrived at. This could mean the physical presence but mental inactivity of a large portion of the class. The breach becomes overt when students read newspapers or fall asleep.

The procedures reported by a teacher or even the class members may not take into account the depth of human feeling about the process. If the teacher asks for evaluations of his process, the student takes what he actually experiences and filters out only what he feels the faculty member wants to know and what may be good for him in that situation. What has been underestimated is the strength of human feelings in the learning process and the importance of establishing a good relationship between those who seek to learn and those who supervise the process. It is easy to rob a student of the joy of a concept that is self-discovered by making a closure on all insights for the class. The extent to which third party materials or ideas are introduced has not yet been fully estimated. Visuals, whether they be films, slides, charts, maps, or pre-programmed resources, such as tapes, records, may reduce or increase the rapport in the learning process depending on the value perceived in them by the learners. If they supplement the sought-for relationships on the part of the learner with human beings who represent the culture he would like to know better, then there is reason to believe that this is wholesome and will enhance the total process.

convergence and self-destiny

There is much ferment concerning the think-alike tendencies required in some courses. No longer are techniques leading to convergent thinking quietly accepted. Student preference for small classes and learning companions who desire freedom of expression are means of avoiding the square box. We do not march into life in classes of twenty but very much alone. The process can replicate life or spin a cocoon.

Perhaps the largest single determiner in the choice of process is the size of the group to be handled. When groups are in the order of hundreds, unless there are multiple teachers, little choice exists but to use the lecture procedure with media support. If the mix of teachers and students can be a lower ratio, alternative procedures are possible. The most underdone resource in higher education is the peer group learning potential. It is used in universities through graduate assistants teaching undergraduates, and is proclaimed as both bane and blessing. The use of undergraduates to help other undergraduates already occurs informally and occurs to a much larger extent when these individuals are urged towards self-instruction. The learning effectiveness of this procedure is questioned, but if it is already occurring, perhaps it could be improved upon by recognizing it and incorporating it in curricular schedules.

In making an analysis of process, one returns to the concept of forward progress in learning. Any group with a common interest and some basic ability can learn from each other, from outside resources, and from a teacher. The organization of this effort to learn is basically the process. The frequent jibe tossed at higher education is "how much you give and how little they take" from class. Groups that use their members to teach each other effectively are the Toastmaster's Clubs, Alcoholics Anonymous, industrial seminars, and psychological therapy teams. The medieval university began by groups of students hiring instructors as they roved from city to city to teach them about their new environment. Occasionally they settled in cities or came to like the instructor and retained him on a more or less permanent basis. Even then it was important that the instructor arrive at the agreed-upon point in the course or that they achieve predetermined competence in the subject.

It seems now that we have gone full circle round and find the student again taking not only interest in but control of his learning situation. This may be long overdue; but it also can be overdone. Basically there is a mutual need to prosper from learning, and when there is a community of interests such as a disaster like a shipwreck, everyone turns to improving his position and possibly the position of all to the extent of his abilities. Those who are interested in a stock investment club, find in owning joint stock that their individual standing is improved. The return to autonomy in the learning situation is one of the heartening yet frightening new directions in higher education.

Courses have been required for so long a time that it is hard to conceive what higher education would be like not having them. Whether this acceptance is the fault of young people or their mentors is hard to ascertain. It is clear that an imposed system exists which has grown out of date. Students want a voluntary system. Some are willing to take on the total process as in the free school. On the other hand some students find relief in having a prescribed program. It should be noted that many people willingly take prescribed courses in the military and business world with good learning outcomes. Many learn how to type without seriously questioning the adequacy of the typewriter keyboard or the techniques that are employed. Process in the sense used here would imply finding place for that unrest, innovation, and evaluation that many students feel uncomfortable without and which have yielded good dividends in the past.

Following the concept of Bloom's *Taxonomy of Educational Objectives,* it would be useful to devise a grouping of processes for learning from the simplest to the most complex. It could be looked at in functional terms and related to the level of ability required by the learner. It could describe in terms of increasing complexity of technique the processes depending only upon the resources within the group to those that depend upon sizable resources in terms of inputs brought to the group. This latter approach will be explored further under the chapter on input.

In summary, the tide is running out upon the uninspected authoritarian processes still imposed through secondary and college programs in the United States. The consequences of the dominance of convergent techniques in these processes is now apparent. A segment of students openly advocates divergent techniques, and a growing number of faculty are prepared to implement them. On this very matter of process, institutions may be split. Those faculty members who prefer the close control of the teaching mode by the faculty group may find institutions to which students are sent by parents who prefer to see their offspring reared in this tradition. Other institutions are already clearly embarked upon another path. They want the student free to gambol and free to fail. Over a period of

years it may become apparent which of these two systems
produced the better group of leaders and thinkers. It may
be that institutional autonomy or the willingness of systems to experiment may become our best source for alternatives in learning procedures.

parameter **4**

the
time relationships

real time and other modes

THERE is now the opportunity to use time in a class experience in many ways. In popular terms the three major choices are live, prerecorded, and deferred use. The setting may be in real time, also called on-line time, in which all that is done and said is by the real life participants as they utter words and perform acts. Another mode provides for preprogrammed materials to be used at will, for interruptions to occur, and on-line discussion to take place as a tape may be interrupted for the purpose of comment. A portion of a lecture can be repeated or skipped or introduced in a different sequence from the original. A variant of these procedures is the "repeat later" procedure by which a lecture, class notes, or tapes can be heard again. Mixing these modes is now quite possible. The storehouse of information from the past as well as the present is tremendous. It presumes a major task of selection and delimitation.

The concept of real time or on-line relationships has

been ushered in by computer programming. With machines able to complete tasks in microseconds, for the first time man is able to obtain an answer within the human expectation of immediately. In fact, it is possible to have a computer solve two men's problems so quickly that both receive answers back which to their human comprehension are immediate and not sequential. With respect to the class learning experience in higher education, on-line means the actual experience of the teacher and that of the student occurring immediately and flowing in a natural time sequence of the actual activities. It is, however, possible to speed up the instructor's speech by means of a spliced audio tape or to show a series of slides in ten seconds that took ten hours or ten years to prepare. This ability to handle a learning experience in terms of past as well as present time modes leads to its description as a dimension that has now become important in higher education. Figure 5 illustrates how time is used in a history class.

Although many time relationships are possible in the classroom, the most frequently used one is that of preprogrammed materials that are reusable in a number of situa-

5.   Time Relationships in a History Class with Media Assistance

9:00   Assemble
9:01   Film clip summary course highlights to date
9:06   Quiz for input levels—(Electronic Response System)
       (Roll taken simultaneously)
9:11   Printout scores—low score items noted
9:13   Refresher material—on low items called up
       Recheck on Electronic Response System—improvement factor
9:16   Outline new material at two levels of achievement
9:18   Common core of material presented—mixed modes
9:38   Short written assignment at two levels
9:47   Post test and printout
9:50   Class dismissed

tions for insertion in the class at a desired time. This is no different from using a film that had been prepared in advance or even the time-honored lecture notes. With much of man's knowledge stored in preprogrammed form, the learning group has at its disposal a wide variety of materials that can be called up on demand, stopped, replayed, or even skipped through. This flexibility in handling the bulk of the materials of a class places a new freedom on all learners in the group. The teacher may be in Europe while his lecture, by video tape, is used by the class. A faculty member may be asleep in bed while the students studying at 2:00 A.M. record over a telephone on tape a question about the last lecture. When the student is sleeping late in the morning, the professor may have gathered these answers and prepared responses to them before the lecture the next day.

It appears likely that learning groups in higher education will choose to mix up their time modes for convenience and individual interest. The concept of continuous progress in which a student takes a course for an indefinite length of time and continues to work at it until a given level of competence is achieved, again breaks down another time constant historically imposed on students. If group learning is to continue in higher education, and students progress at different rates, then some accommodation to those things that can best be done together and those which can conveniently be done individually must be made. Backup systems can fill in missed lectures, and the inconvenience of distance can easily be bridged by technology. What appears likely is that the mixed time mode will continue because it is a convenient and efficient feature of higher education.

time, reality, and truth

Until the present it was not possible to relive much of the learning experience after it had happened. Now with tape recordings the only limit seems to be the cost of storage and an efficient indexing and retrieval system. The learning experience is more than just the hour spent together as a class. Students reflect on what has been said and also prepare in advance for what is said. It is also true that students bring to the learning environment a number of experiences acquired in the past which are frequently relived in the present. An encounter with an authority figure may bring out the resentment once held toward a father. Ways to solve a problem and a style of life may persist long after the artificial group, called a class, ceases to function as such. The grade only measures what has been achieved within a limited time span and is not a good indication of what will occur in the future. The time boundaries of the learning experience are difficult to define.

The real time mode is so natural we use it without thinking of it as a mode. It is as automatic as breathing and as invisible as the air we catch in the process. When we stop to think of an automatic process we see it afresh. Real time is such a concept.

We can choose the best mode for our purpose. Sounds of World War II or even pictures of the Civil War are familiar ways of stepping out of the present time. However, the use or reuse of materials from ancient or previous times is not new or spectacular. We have used charts, maps, and more recently records and pictures that represent a brief event or accumulation of what has occurred in the past. Never are they the dominant mode. They are introduced as a point of contrast or departure. The better analogy would be to reenact a session of the Continental Congress. More interesting still would be to reenact it as an evening at the theater. Even that would be a small part of the whole of what happens in real time because the earlier materials are used for comparison only.

The ground zero or the datum level for classroom time relationships is definitely the contemporary. Yet, in a sense, all that is done in the class is for the future. Although there is some transitory pleasure in learning, and this may be an end in itself, most of it is prolegomena or beginning for a successive lesson or a life experience. The on-line experience is seldom pure in the aesthetic sense meaning unalloyed with past or present meaning and materials. The sequential nature of learning condemns it to be seen as time present. The whole process of recall has for its purpose relating what went before to our ability to solve more complex contemporary problems. In summary, to act in a more self-sufficient manner has the seed of the past in it.

Much of the sparkle of on-line experiences comes from the immediacy of persons. When you remove the persons from the immediate vicinity of each other or introduce a video connection, the fullness of the other person is lost. The portion lost is the spontaneity of response that as yet can not be substituted for by a preprogrammed computer. Distance has fallen easy prey to this innovation; however, time is a little harder. Homework and lectures themselves are part of previous work introduced in class. It is only the delivery of the homework or the presentation of the lecture that is in real time.

The substitution of the instructor in another time mode than his actual presence can only be faulted for the lack of feedback or possibly the feeling that the instructor is not giving personal attention to this group. The same might be true for an instructor facing rows of tape recorders instead of students for his lecture.

When a student response system is coupled to a computer, the turn-around time between posing a question and receiving answers from all in the group is much less than the time for an individual student to answer verbally. Although this is a bit disconcerting to the teacher, the questions can be analyzed for validity, and statistical tests of the sufficiency of the items can be made on-line so that changes can be made immediately in any further questions. Using the same type of response system with discussion, the full opinion of the class can be displayed to the class and the responses compared with stored data so that more information is available to both student and class within seconds than either may be able to assimilate easily. What occurs is the opportunity to modify at each level of the ongoing learning experience the next level by full analysis of what has occurred. Not all participants in the learning situation, including the teacher, are prepared to face the awful moment of truth about defective test questions or answers without time to think of an alternative.

flexibility and control

Although the mentor of the past has been the instructor, the mentor of the future may be the accumulated wisdom of a quick retrieval system. Libraries have been with us for some time, but to search through them for answers comes much later than the class incident in which either the student or the teacher is faced with data that do not support his point of view. This may force the teacher into the role of guide or assistant to the learning process more than answer-giver and judge. The process is still a complicated one, and not only the guiding hand but the authoritative hand is often wanted.

In counseling, in training men to fly, and in registration, the preprogrammed instruction to students that has been stored in a computer seems to work as well as instructions from a live instructor. Whatever ambiance remains by having the person immediately available will have to be judged in terms of the larger resources available through impersonal approaches. Air travel reservations are booked by a computer; weather forecasts are tapes dialed up by telephone. Problems may be accumulated and answered sufficiently quickly in a media linkage that it seems plausibly personal. Seeing an individual on closed-circuit television is only a partial answer to those with warm emotional relationships and who want to express them.

With increased ability to connect visually remote participants in the learning process, non-real time modes become easier to accept. Video is certainly one of the techniques and the computer the other. For simple lecture material, directions, or quizzes, a preprogrammed presentation is just about as easy to use as the on-line experience.

With short message handling, such as by tape retrieval system or electronic secretary, the short delay between message in and message back is quite acceptable. Telegraph preceded telephone with the short delay and the intermediary telegraph operator. We even see benefits in short delay if the system completes a larger task in response to a query. For example, the reservation service of airlines provides a means of quick exchange of information and a transaction not quite in real-time but sufficiently close that we don't notice the difference.

There are many advantages to out-of-real-time learning elements. Many more hours of preparation can go into it than a live presentation as, for example, a good short color film or closed film loop. It can be run at any speed, stopped, started, or reversed, or otherwise manipulated to produce a more acceptable reaction. Not least important is the chance to talk and react honestly to the material while it is being presented. This would be awkward in the presence of the author.

Some people like to review their performance before they give it to improve it. It also makes the presentation available to others if placed in media channels. Good examples find imitators, and all are informed. This dimension need be further explored with respect to how to make the intermix so realistic that learning is maximized —and the concern for what is real and what is canned becomes of secondary importance.

By mixed mode is meant the meaningful interrelation of time modes so that the overall learning effect is not dependent on what is available from live performers all the time. Some of the advantages include: the use of library resources in video as well as written form, the late night or otherwise out-of-regular-time use of materials, the programming of the best combination of resources regardless of the immediate availability of the person.

This technique of mixed mode should apply not only to the teacher's management of the course but also to the students and their participation in the learning setting. Students find substitutes for themselves and, without their real presence, still have a meaningful experience. This is done in part now when a student uses a friend's notes or a tape recorder. It occurs also when an educational message handling telephone service is used. A professor grades a class quiz and finds that the students have missed one of the points in his lecture. He can tape for a telephone retrieval system comments about the test and suggestions for further study. Students then dial in for this message and raise further questions. These questions may be collected on the tape, read by the professor the following morning, preparing him to respond to the class at its next session.

The parameter of the time relationship in the collegiate learning experience is the mode of real-time. Perhaps 90 percent of what is done in the classroom occurs in real-time. Most of the remaining 10 percent is taken up by pre-programmed lecture materials and taped instructional materials in learning centers. The trend is encouraging although it is a long way from a majority movement. With more efficient storage of instructional material, preprogramming, and deferred usage, snapshot as well as time exposure approaches are feasible. Taped audio materials take so little time and pose so little threat that many community colleges have some such materials in every required course. These stored materials may well parallel the library books of yesteryear as the major source of instructional help and shift the parameter of the time relationship from real-time to a mixed mode.

One of the great disproportions with respect to the time relationship is the relatively slow rate at which a student can make visual signals back compared to the rate multimedia in the hands of the teacher can be thrust at him. For the most part he is still limited to spoken or written responses which are no match for the broad display systems available to the teacher. Language itself is a slow and halting symbolic tool compared to the motion-picture film. It is true that a teacher observes the reaction of class

members; and in very small classes, dialogue can be frequent. What is needed it seems is a new type of shorthand
or means by which people can communicate in symbolic
form without the human voice. Man has always drawn
pictures, but this also is slow. If those engaged in the
learning process could have at their command ten to fifty
thousand symbols typed out by an electronic console not
as letters of the alphabet nor even as notes on the scale of
an electronic organ but as an idea-bank topically and systematically arranged, it is conceivable that communication between two individuals might be enhanced. Ballet,
pantomime, and the improvisation at happenings show
that much can be transmitted in symbolic form. With the
aid of an electronic storage unit and indexing so that
quick retrieval could be obtained, the time lag in expressing ideas could be shortened.

As to future directions of the time relationship, it is
evident that modern man has the ability to use accumulated as well as contemporary data and mix them to make
a meaningful and realistic package. The process is not
really new. Charts, maps, and other types of stored summaries have long been used. Memory is an internal time-
switcher upon which we depend for checks on where
we are. How to tag the kind of time used is still a puzzle.
More needs to be learned about recall for it is a most important part of our learning process. The analogy of history as a hinged gate may not seem so descriptive in the
future.

The on-line syndrome of some of today's students poses
a problem. They may be turned on, tuned in, and amaz-
ingly relevant to today only. It is hard for them to conceive of a generation to follow who will think that they

botched up their youth as much as this generation thinks the older one did. This time displacement in the social orientation of at least some of today's students may be an appropriate epilogue to the fresh look many of us hope for in the time relationship of the learning experience.

parameter **5**

inputs to
the learning situation

identifying the inputs

TIIE four previously mentioned dimensions—the complement of persons, the space used, the process involved, and
the time relationships—all relate to the learning experience as a whole. Taken as a group they represent the four
major dimensions of the learning matrix and provide a
sufficient basis to describe each experience uniquely. The
next three—inputs, interactions, and outputs—together
represent the dynamics of the mid-length collegiate learning experience. Each will be taken up in a separate
chapter.

The learning situation has as one of its major dimensions a cluster of inputs or resources brought to it by all
those who participate. The teacher takes on the formal role
of supplying textbooks, lecture materials, assignments,
and a style of format for the classroom which is often arbitrary. Certainly the learning is influenced and often enhanced by the materials introduced. The students also

bring many years of experience and even certain expectations usually blown to them on the winds of rumor from previous students. In addition to the persons involved, the enclosure may facilitate access to resources although not properly classified as an input in itself. The range of this dimension may be thought of in terms of the subscales of few to many, or in terms of the mix, or in terms of the descriptive nature of the input. Figure *6* identifies the major sources of input.

6. Classification and Measurement of Inputs

Kinds of Input	Examples of Kind	Quantitative Scale
Teacher brought	Subject Knowledge	low yield to high yield
	Time Consciousness	casual to demanding
Student brought	Secondary school recall	low to high yield
	Concept of fairness	hostile to cooperative
Group Initiated	Building a model	low participation to high participation
	Preparing a protest	low participation to high participation
Space held	Classroom library	low use to high use
	Tour of computing center	low interest to high interest
Externally introduced	TV news items	irrelevant to relevant
	Computer responses	irrelevant to relevant
Recycling (processed inputs become further inputs)	Using the model for experiment	inefficient to efficient
	Student summaries of discussion	not useful to useful

The use of some of these resources is almost inescapable. For example, each participant has a memory that he uses just to recall his name or the names of other participants. Beyond the personal resources through the memory and experience of each participant are those resources introduced either purposely or accidentally that stand apart from the ones inherently a part of the participants. Even Mark Hopkins and his eager student on the log had many inputs besides the world of nature about them.

The variety and richness of these inputs vary by tangibility, reproducibility, and general or specific ownership. Educators are concerned with the quantitative nature of inputs as a first step to measuring outputs and incremental change. Although tests are still an imperfect instrument they are increasingly used to assign students to class sections and to give some estimate of the progress that might be expected. In some institutions of higher education placement in a more-advanced or less-advanced section is based upon the record contained in grades and tests. The profile of freshmen now entering a university is known both on an institutional and national level, and this in formation is often known to the student as well.

It is quite a distance both in time and complexity from the hornbook of the New England school to the multimedia classroom learning space today. Not only is more hard-copy input available such as text books, films, records, and tapes, but also devices that facilitate resource utilization such as computers and calculators, not to mention the more common devices such as blackboards and projectors. Grouping these resources and noting their impact is the purpose of this chapter. It is difficult to know where to put the moral integrity of a student. It might be thought of as a resource or input for a class. If it is lacking, the teacher must provide certain safeguards to award grades fairly. Motivation and concern for others are also inputs.

Let the inputs be divided into several categories: those already contained within the teacher as factual knowledge or past experience; those held by the student in memory or experience; outside resources such as visitors, texts, hard-copy resources such as books, films, records, and tapes; a cluster of devices that are means to resources such as calculators, projectors, and computers; and other resources such as those created in the class itself.

teacher and student inputs

Historically the teacher has been the richest input resource the class had. Should the teacher be ill the class was dismissed, and only on rare occasions would it meet on its own without having a substitute teacher. With the increasing self-actualization of advance-level students, a seminar can be continued without the instructor. The teacher provides a style which includes tension, urging students to learn, as well as a certain amount of factual material and authority with respect to answers. Encouragement may be given, insights shared, or assistance with experiments provided. The so-called "bag of tricks" of the teacher may be called upon to provide the necessary incentives or dynamic environment to assure the student's forward progress.

Increasingly the student holds the balance of power in the classroom and develops earlier in life more varied inputs than the previous generation. He is more verbal, more widely traveled, and less beholden to authority. The impersonality of today's society acts as a deterrent to his easy acceptance of a colleague in class as a trusted friend; however, some sharing of inputs continues. He, like the teacher, has a wide variety of past experiences available through memory, and habit patterns as well as a cluster of friends, a few textbooks and previous notes. To some extent the learning process becomes a matter of rearrangement of existing inputs more than always introducing new ones. This leads to discussion of already-known issues, the reduction of prejudice, and the newer task of helping the teacher understand the way the student thinks about the world "that really is." In spite of the widely reported student revolution most classes still require the student to produce written work for the teacher's review and only a limited opportunity for the students to determine the procedures in class.

In addition to the teacher and student, this category will identify other human inputs than the ones supplied directly by the teacher and the class. This would include visiting experts, the sights and sounds that come into a classroom from a laboratory or outside world, and increasingly the immediate events that make an impact upon the world of the classroom in terms of news that is happening. Awareness in a college group of the many things happening has been increased by the communication facilities available, and it tempers the discussions in many classes.

environmental inputs

The great spurt forward in the last decade has been in hard-copy materials available to the class. The library with its books has long been such a resource; however, by electronic switching pictorial and sound materials are available even more conveniently to those in the class. These become potential inputs if not actual ones during the session. In fact, with the enclosure not always easily identified as a classroom, the place where the resource is used may not be the classroom itself. An increasing number of resources are available by telephone, by tape in carrels, and in a variety of other ways. Within the classroom itself, processing devices like photocopy machines, and small libraries make inputs and the processing of inputs a natural thing.

Of substantial power and great future importance is the computer and other devices which can calculate or become the means to process existing inputs. Classes in journalism have available a wire service news printer and many classes in business, engineering, and the physical sciences have computer terminals available for students as well as faculty for calculations. Progress has been made in a dozen or more institutions with computer-aided instruction and the single concept closed loop film projector has added simulated motion to pictorial information in a very handy form. What can be said in general is that we may now be using more inputs in a class than ever, and that many of these inputs are not from the teacher himself but are scheduled or programmed by him.

As a class progresses, some of its inputs are processed and made outputs then used again for further processing and a second set of outputs. In one sense these class-generated outputs which in turn become inputs must be looked at as a complex network. For example, a class may be asked to participate in an evaluation of some material recently covered. The result of the class's deliberation becomes an input for the test that is given later. This makes it difficult, except by looking at the learning situation at one instant of time, to easily separate what might be called an input and what is called an output. As a sequel to the nonfaculty-generated inputs that now predominate in classes is the class-created inputs now possible in moderate-sized classroom situations. This comes about through stu-rent-oriented learning situations and the greater general level of activity of students in the learning environment. It runs at a very high level when preprogrammed materials are given, or in general when students are placed in individual learning situations but have the availability of a group leader for comment and occasional group participation.

Still another category of inputs are the exotic ones. In some class learning situations such as a world trip or a free school, the inputs are more casual and unstructured. Contemplation, rapping, or ritual become ways to open the mind to inputs that might otherwise escape them. These exotic efforts occasionally prove fruitful, and the input is often entirely apart from a specific teacher. Experiences of young people in the service or world travel in general have given them cultural shock and raise the question about total immersion as a satisfactory total input.

the input explosion

When many of our institutions of higher education were founded a hundred or more years ago, the small library and the solitary professor provided most of the inputs for his students. Today the flood of materials must be selected and limited if frustration is to be avoided. Finding relevant materials becomes in itself a major job of assessment. What are the educational advantages of increased use of input resources? This basic philosophical question is often unasked and more often unanswered. If these inputs are to free the student to pursue learning on his own, they have yet to be evaluated for this purpose. If they are to allow those who are most able to proceed at a faster rate, then questions are raised about the group process as a whole. It has opened the door to the possibility of a much larger portion of the student's time being used at the individual's own rate and level of interest. This range of inputs forms another kind of continuum from the one extreme of the mimeographed outline of the course to the judgment of the teacher in giving a grade. A second scale might indicate the level of richness that students really enjoy. One could use so many inputs that the teacher is simply a manager or stage director for the many activities, or the teacher might use them sparingly keeping most of the focus upon his own management of the student's own resources. This raises the question about the students becoming a passive group if they are flooded with inputs.

The richness of inputs in terms of flexibility, versatility, and sheer quantity is with civilized man from now on. Ever since he moved to an urban environment and began accumulating the record of his past experience and much about his present, he surrounded himself with a jungle of inputs, more than he can manage. It is a monument to his cultural affluence, his tenacious hold on the past, the rich dividends of scientific inquiry, and his endless quest for individuality. It is now being preserved and catalogued, but most important of all it is easy to retrieve, and worst of all it can be automatically copied. The problem of selection itself becomes monumental.

Richness raises the question of selectivity, and selectivity raises the question of criteria. It may be that the teacher of the future will be known for his apt selection of learning resource inputs rather than for any flair or style of his own delivery.

perspectives

Beyond collating the great wealth of inputs now available lies the prospect of creating better inputs, perhaps going full circle round to have the live teacher become still more important not only as programmer but as a major participant. The student must decide how to use this great wealth of input resources. Television alone has made it possible for the great majority of the people in the western world to learn about a place or problem through media before confronting it personally. We travel today to confirm what media inputs have already told us.

If a parameter can be described for the category of inputs, it would be one of equilibrium between too much and too little by way of inputs. Previous generations suffered from a paucity of resources. Tomorrow's child will be flooded with them. The paperback revolution multiplied the printed word; television vulgarized audio visual symbols; and the automobile gave the majority great mobility. These mark this century through the sixties as a time of mass distribution of inputs. The seventies should see this plethora of inputs stored, codified, evaluated, and probably franchised.

parameter **6**

interaction in
the learning setting

the nature of interaction

THERE is a transdirectional aspect to the learning situation that is often identified in terms of feedback, transference, and interrelationships. Teachers are constantly sending signals to students, and students are signaling back. Subtle signs as nodding of assent, showing interest by alertness in the eye, raising the hand to pose a question, or contributing verbally without such a signal are means students have used to make the interchange more nearly equal. For years this feedback has been noticed by other members of the learning group. Only recently has information about it been formally and systematically collected. Some of the feedback such as note taking or speaking to a classmate are only partially known to the group. After defining the input, the interaction is thought to be what happens in between the input and the final consequence or output.

The process most frequently used in higher education

learning situations, the lecture, has so characterized the whole process that we think of the teacher normally presenting information and occasionally letting the students feed back some response. Actually a much more nearly two-way process is envisioned as the better way for learning to take place. If a freer two-way exchange is allowed, some means of channeling to keep the group moving forward or preventing it from breaking into subdiscussion groups is essential. Until recently there was no way to do this; however, the technology now exists to let groups interact at two or even three levels within the same general space envelope. Problems may arise for an individual in attempting to follow two or three kinds of data input at the same time, and more studies need to be made as to the ability of man to adapt to a complex world full of sensory signals.

In addition to the overt means of feedback there are the covert ways. An example is the passive resistance a classmate gives the teacher in responding to a question to which only a few of his fellow students know the answer. Those who know it do not want to expose the ignorance of the rest of the class by making answer to it. When ideas are exciting in a class, students react in many ways to show their interest other than verbally. It may be tactual or just a general excitement level as a whole. If the opportunity for anonymous responses, as in a student response system, is provided, a whole new level of concern is expressed, sometimes overstated and critical but basically genuine. An animosity can develop in a class that may be hidden and only expressed in subtle fashion such as satire or diversion techniques. Few teachers know how to cope with it so they tolerate it or squelch it. Those who dare to expose it find it painful but rewarding. A communication link is opened, and a certain amount of trust is exchanged. This partial block to free exchange of feeling as well as factual data contains the great hope for the next generation. The techniques exist to deal with it. It will take an act of faith between two generations.

There often is a lively interplay between students in addition to the feedback to the teacher. One of the reasons for having the group together is to allow for this interaction in addition to any efficiencies that come by having the group use common resources. If the teacher uses the lecture technique, there is a portion of the mental activity of each student not given just to receiving the lecturing information but in note taking, question formation, and group interaction. This takes place at the subtle level of students noticing one another's actions and from that deciding how they themselves should react. This ability of a group to visual back to each other is still a little-understood technique.

Any student cringing in his seat waiting for the teacher to ask him to recite when not fully prepared is a reminder of our own experience and the emotional stress it caused. The ability of a teacher to keep interest and attention by eye contact is also a subtle procedure. This is a finely tuned feedback system we have developed. There has been no other way until recently by which it could be done. Our visuling back system is subtle but limited to what our body can manipulate by pantomime, touch, or a small written output. The range of the body might be extended by hardware to make broader and more versatile these symbolic actions. A hand control panel that has keys and even a memory, and possibly the availability of a small store of pictures that could be used by individual members to communicate in a dialogue simultaneously, would be useful in group meetings such as classes and in other situations as well. Two people sketching as they talk is a primitive example of this.

multilevel feedback

Interaction may be multilevel in that a total group can hear at one sound level while a subgroup can hear a second message at a lower level. The same principle applies to visuals with the additional freedom that two visuals can be of equal strength. An example of two-level audio reception is a lecture going on while several people whisper or all whisper so there is a buzz among the class. Today small groups watching a television program and listening to the sound also talk with each other adjusting the volume of the television audio to allow themselves to speak and yet not miss what is being broadcast. Some people complain of strain when attempting to concentrate on two messages simultaneously. Others find it exciting.

With increased use of two sound paths reaching the individual, studies are underway to find what interference patterns are at work and how multiple sound paths can be effectively accommodated. The television commentator with the small earphone in his ear is able to speak while receiving private sound information. Foreign visiting groups by using a similar device can hear a simultaneous translation of a speaker in one ear and in the other, the original. This same principle applied to two levels could allow a group of learners to communicate with each other while still hearing the voice of the teacher. Another variant of this is to have, by throat mikes, the questions of the students directed to an assistant to the teacher who could relay them, in large class situations, by writing or otherwise to the teacher who would insert the responses in the consequent flow of lecture material.

One can think of many ways to accommodate the flow of lecture materials to the reactions of students. In the class break technique the teacher stops, allows the group to discuss in total or in small discussion groups, and then has them come back for further materials. In the continuous session he allows a one-to-one exchange by answering questions from the class with the unfortunate ratio of many listeners and few speakers. In the prerecorded technique now possible with preprogrammed material, he lets lecture material be interrupted and then, by class majority agreement, a part is repeated, skipped over, or supplemented.

Little thought is now being given to more than two aural pathways, although recent military experience indicates that some individuals have been able to hear four or five simultaneous messages in dealing with aircraft operations. A common experience when a friend is talking on the telephone, and you ask if he would let you talk to the person to whom he is talking when he finishes, will usually be that he will hang up and then ask you what you said. This inability to receive two messages is a part of our concentration skill that has proved useful in the past. Many students today study with music or other background materials, and there is evidence to show that random noise or other means of washing out background disturbances may actually aid concentration. It is even exciting to have two related streams of sound coming at us simultaneously. At least we enjoy stereophonic music.

complex visual interactions

With the rise of television's coverage of football games, the passer and receiver being placed side by side on the screen has become a familiar juxtaposition. The physical concept of space is secondary to the interest in the outcome of a pass thrown. This ability to join cause and consequence in a symbolic representation in real time has come late in man's history but with good purpose. A small device on the table between two people could actuate simultaneously complex symbols more quickly than two voices could. It would make it possible for people to communicate more rapidly and at a greater depth. The simultaneous or rapidly sequented use of visuals is with us to stay. It may be as old as the fact that dogs traveling in packs had to be aware of one another through peripheral vision. Through some fortunate early history man acquired the ability to see several things at the same time. The very fact that we have binocular vision and can perceive depth leads to the supposition that man seeing two separate images has learned to see them simultaneously and learned from their difference a perception of depth. Although the phenomenon is not fully understood and represents a delicate balance of two eyes, the wide-angle of vision of man makes it possible to see a complex array of symbolic representations at one time.

That reading becomes one of our quickest means of assimilating data, as well as that of visualizing pictures, is no accident. That a large percentage of the energy of our bodies is absorbed in eye movement is also not unusual, nor is the large concentration of nerve endings. Studies of total information units through our sensory system show that the eye is by far the most prolific receptor. It may then be that the visual route will be the first way to accept multiple images in meaningful constellations.

creative uses of interaction

Interaction in learning involves all our senses and all the people. The seating arrangment in a class affects people's relationships and to quote Einstein, "sitting on a hot stove makes a minute seem like an hour, but having a pretty girl on your lap makes an hour seem like a minute." Interpersonal reactions either within the class or preceding it affect the class rapport and progress. Too often class members are competitors for a limited number of good grades which are related to the expectations of the teacher and which are also related to the individual's own interests. Students are affected by temperature, humidity, air flow, and a variety of other room conditions. In higher education the most important interchange concerns concepts and ideas. The ability to interact and shape these concepts is the purpose of most learning situations. Occasionally there is a tangible output, such as the successful completion of an experiment, but even that is a specific means of enhancing insight and appreciation.

If a group of students were allowed to devise a learning situation in which they would feel most creative or free to interact and learn, one wonders what it might be. The first suggestion is freedom to select the learning materials and the free choice of those to assist with the learning process. It might also include selection of colleagues and the environment. Assuming seriousness of purpose, the class would ask for modest library resources and generous opportunity for their ideas to be heard and reviewed. The students would like even more time to speak than their prorata share among colleagues. They would like the expertise of the teacher held back, asking him to listen while they had a chance to explore on a trial and error basis ideas with which they were just then becoming familiar. This would be a rich student-oriented environment. It would maximize learning. It is more descriptive of the honor section than it is of the free school, although both have elements of it in them.

Several arguments can be given for the values that accrue from interaction during the learning period. It is natural for human beings to communicate and to signal back and forth. In an authoritarian environment a leader directs the followers in the way he wants with the most able keeping up with the teacher and the other falling behind. In that sense it becomes a screening procedure. If the intent is not to eliminate some of the class but to enhance learning for all, then a moderate amount of interaction should occur at least enough to keep the group together. If the intention is to help each learn at his maximum rate, then a special but limited kind of interaction is meaningful for the most able students and a generous but different amount for the least able. Most of us have seen classes in which generous amounts of interaction took place, but there was uncertainty about the outcomes. There is much more to be learned about the contribution of interaction to the total experience.

Several examples of interesting efforts to achieve interaction in the learning process are underway. At the Harvard School of Business Administration telephones by student chairs in a carpeted and acoustically damped lecture hall allow individuals to call an assistant to the professor to raise questions or furnish information. Student re-

sponse systems are located in many universities including
Syracuse, Southern Illinois, and San Diego State. In many
schools with learning resource centers, group carrels have
been devised in which the students can talk with each
other while the presentation is sufficiently loud that it
can be heard over general conversation.

The implications of these efforts to provide for interaction are clear. It has become more overt and frequent
and as a result better recognized and managed. The space
envelope can accommodate many styles aided by technology. Responses to instructional evaluation inquiries indicate that students want more interaction. Teachers no
longer command the position of unassailable respect and
omniscience if they ever really did. In general the climate is right for a careful look at these interactions and a
wider and more effective use of them.

The parameter for interaction in the learning setting
has been, until recently, faculty control. In European universities students still stand to recite and professorial decisions are seldom questioned. The most frequent interaction in such an environment has been to speak only
when invited to and in practice not to speak too much.
This parameter has permitted a larger number of idiosyncrasies in teachers, endearing in many cases but also a
blunt testimony to their veto power. Not just the responses but learning itself was directed by the teacher.
Grades, assistantships, and recommendations held the student in thrall. The separation of the university from the
civil authority also encouraged this separate justice, and
the fortunate 10 percent of the population favored by
family or ability to attend the university were sternly directed for in turn they would have to assume major re-
sponsibilities for regulating others.

Today the parameter has become the satisfaction of the student who now is the customer. Minority groups insist on being called Sir or Miss, and records of achievement may not be divulged without approval. Faculty members can be required to show cause why a student did not pass; and the pass/fail grade blunts the scimitar of faculty imposed grades. The impact of the changed status of students affects interactions in the learning situation. It provides for more honest exchanges and now tends toward the climate of an adversary system instead of the former collegiate one. The exchange is more equal, and the settlement of differences is by due process. The door to the classroom is more often open so that third party observation is more common. Those who love to teach and teach effectively are well regarded. They now enjoy a responsive audience.

parameter 7

the outputs of
the learning situation

the consequence

THE consequence or output of the learning experience,
using the normal class period as a module, is a complex
achievement. There is an immediate gain particularly in
factual information that can be measured by a test given
in the last minutes of the hour. There are concepts that
have been glimpsed or understood for the first time. They
may be remembered for a longer time than the factual
information and used as tools in new situations. If Dewey
is right that ideas are instruments that we use in our social situation, the understanding and shaping of these
tools can occur during class and have a very lasting effect.
There is also the affective output in which changes in
attitudes occur, either toward one's self, other members of
the class, the teacher, or society in general. In addition to
new information, a class period is used for reflection.
When that which was spoken of in class is compared with
what was already known, new and old concepts are min-

gled in so complex a fashion that cause and consequence are not easily diagnosed. The mere fact that man's process of learning is most intricate and elusive should not be a deterrent to further attempts at systematic analysis.

Setting aside for the moment the latent effects and concentrating upon those that are immediate, what are some of the more specific ones? In most cases there is a set of notes or marginal comments upon an outline that was handed out. It often becomes the agenda for the class period as well as a scheduling device. Another piece of hard copy is the test or quiz. It is frequently given at the beginning of the "next" period but not given often enough as a comparison between what the student knew at the beginning of the hour and what he knew at the end. If, however, pre and posttesting are used, a better estimate of incremental learning can be made. Discussions can often lead to strong polarization of opinion, and a student may leave a class angry or confused. Later he understands a point he was not able to before. There is also the possibility of oversell in which after hearing a very persuasive argument for one side, he is completely convinced until attending either another class or talking with friends or just letting the aura wear off. Then he returns to a moderate or reversed position. In mathematics, language, and other types of sequential subjects, it is possible to see the incremental gain of one class as part of a larger total because the graded set of educational tasks or problems is in a quantitative sequence.

The latent effect of the learning experience is hard, if at all possible, to relate to a specific antecedent. If able minds learn in spite of teachers, or putting it perhaps better, if it is hard to keep able minds from thinking of all the possibilities that there are, the class may only happen to be the place in which the student's free mind does most of its own inquiry and decision making. This is an indirect way of saying that not all of the class material is relevant or well fashioned. That students learn in spite of the teachers has been a marvel in the field of education for centuries. We identify much of current class activity in the direction of conformity and convergent thinking. Does this tend to bend all minds alike? Apparently not, for at the same time there is a groundswell causing creativity or divergent thinking. While starting with the same premises in class a surprisingly large number will end up with different conclusions and find encouragement to do so.

It is clear that the intended outcomes as viewed by society, legislators, faculties, and students differ. Each has his way of measuring the outcome of a single class or of the total experience. Society and those representing it in the legislature, tend to look at the long-term effect, except when they get concerned about some particular teaching incident that does not fit their general, social, or moral codes. Faculty and students tend to look at outcomes in terms of social consequence also, which is primarily grades for the students and professional status for the faculty member. The research-oriented teacher seeks the opportunity to use the class as a seedbed for ideas, a testing ground, or the source of further ideas. If the student could have a comfortable experience yet learn something useful, in general he is pleased. The total class reaction is often the sum of many divergent opinions of what should happen. The recent trend to having students evaluate the learning experience, usually as a total course sequence, has been a long-awaited breath of fresh air. Faculty members occasionally analyze their own class outputs with subjec-

tive or objective evaluation forms. The reports differ but
not radically. Good teaching is recognized by all groups,
and most often the various constituencies note the same
reasons.

the direct consequences

In many fields the direct consequence or output can be
measured. A teacher can review by tape or other technique
how far or how well the material has been presented. This
can even be evaluated by a group of peers or by the class
itself. The students in terms of their demonstrated achievement can show what they have learned, particularly in
terms of subject content. In addition to measuring knowledge elements, measuring attitudinal change is possible.
The basic competitive nature of the higher education
process in which only the ablest students go on, makes the
output measure a screening device for employment by
business, industry, and government.

Most higher education learning experiences depend
upon some quantitative measure of achievement. The
usual pattern is to require several out-of-class assignments,
several in-class tests, and a final examination. Some evaluation is placed upon recitation, discussion, and laboratory
achievement. The quality of these performances is usually
translated into a quantitative measure either in percent
or a letter grade and then accumulated to give a grade for
the course. Occasionally a faculty member will write an
appraisal of the student's achievement in essay form as
well. This grade is frequently the only measure of the
student's work in that course. That it is based upon limited
segments of the total learning experience and an arbitrary

quantification of a qualitative process is occasionally up-braided in the literature, but little is done about it. Most teachers strive for better methods of evaluating class members, and there are many articles about class curve and the insufficiency of the grading procedure.

The use of grading as a device to select from higher education those most approved for society's most responsible jobs or for further training is of ancient origin. It must be admitted that the grading procedure influences the process too, and that one of the purposes of a student is to succeed in the course almost at all cost. This invites cheating, diagnosing what the teacher wants and meeting the teacher's requirements, or even playing upon the teacher's weaknesses or preferences. Many students try to play it straight, but it cannot be denied that grading does influence what happens in the classroom. This coupled with required attendence makes the experience a kind of servitude to which many students object. Voluntary systems have not been effective, and the experiments with pass/fail grade, currently popular, do not give very clear delineations of ability. In spite of the onerous nature of grading, most people prefer to see it continued, particularly those who are most able and who are usually most vocal and influential.

It is becoming increasingly clear that interpersonal relationships are an important part of the evaluative outcomes. Phrases such as "teacher's pet" describe efforts to influence a teacher's evaluation by student cunning. We have come to think of the relationships as the norm, whether they be currying favor or exercising discipline. The more natural and general relationship of people liking and understanding each other has not been as care-

fully reviewed. The large potential benefits in these interpersonal relationships is to increase a total effort of the
class and thereby improve its total production. If rewards
are limited, students fight for them both by achievement
but also by disrupting others. Part of the interest in pass/
fail grades stems from a natural quest for the limited number of good grades. A class can become a functioning
group early in the semester's experience and can achieve
much more than one that has never been allowed to form
its own identity and have its own values understood.

The outcomes of the learning experience are both immediate and long term. They are also theoretical and practical. A class experience may be the most recent in a series
of formative events which cause a major change in a person's life. A dislike for a course or a person may change
over time and become far more favorable as the benefits
of the learning become related to later experience. In one
sense the outcome of the educational experience is the
development of a style in life, which occurs in hundreds
of places and experiences and is formed by the person into
an overall direction only after a certain latent period.

It is much easier to measure the practical outcomes of
the course which are often quantitative rather than the
theoretical or ideational. The trouble is more with our
means of measuring the outcomes than in the reality of
the outcome itself. Factual knowledge and skills such as
computational ability or laboratory technique are tangible
and easily measurable in terms of incremental improvement. The understanding of a concept, the relationship
between a principle and its application are not so easy to
identify and evaluate. Both kinds of outcomes are necessary and desirable. Perhaps the best example of outcome

measurement is in programmed learning books where
short incremental steps are accumulated so that the net
effect becomes evident.

the indirect consequences

From every class experience there is at least the possibility
that there will be indirect output. By this is meant the
tangential products of the experience. One might develop
a great hatred for the subject or fall in love with it. These
might be considered more or less direct; however, while
a class is in session a student may be sparked by an idea
only remotely related to the class, but for him it becomes
of major consequence. The ability of a class to stimulate
divergent thinking is part of the justification of the class
method itself. If people are to learn in a group, then all
must be able to proceed alike, for the format is created in
which people who are inherently different find enough in
common to receive materials simultaneously. Then, after
assimilating them, they use them in different ways for different outputs. A wise teacher might expect this divergence in output and be prepared to evaluate progress for
each not upon a uniform basis but one that takes into account the individual differences in the class.

It may be impossible to insulate the personality effects
of a class from its content and subject orientation. Human
personality is shaped by these encounters in an intellectual
environment. If one studies in a philosophy course about
moral decision making, it is likely that such a person will
apply some of this knowledge to his life and his own goals
and motivations. Phillip Jacob's study of changing values
in college showed that few were really changed, on the
other hand the potential for change as well as the actual

change may be two different measures. It is likely, however, that people's personalities do change both with respect to each other, the teacher, and the external environment. This cannot be overlooked as an effect of the class experience, although it is not one for which a grade is given nor one for which the teacher can judge an impact. Each college undergraduate commits himself to a major at about the midpoint of his undergraduate career. This decision is not shaped entirely by home or even by colleagues. Most likely it has been formed by class experiences and the student's relationship to them.

Earlier the envelope for the class was defined as a semipermeable membrane which had the effect of letting more come into the class than pass out. Today multimedia can let in much that has been preprogrammed not just through TV screens, but through recreation of reality. On the other hand there is some movement from the inside to the outside that should not be overlooked. Each student shaped by the course moves outside the class experience to affect others by telling a classmate, acting according to a new insight, or in general making his impact not only on himself, but society.

other consequences
of the learning situation

Another effect of the learning experience that has become common recently is the effort of students to change the very process of which they are a part. This self-introspection about the procedure has surprised many in the academic community. At present it is directed more to means than ends, but it is likely to be concerned with ends in the long run. In general students and even some faculty mem-

bers have not been fully a part of the total higher education effort, and their interest in the ends as well as the
means will be a continuing concern. This consequence of
the learning process is salutary. The thoughtful, insightful
student is not content merely to be processed but judges
the process even while he is being judged.

The time is right in terms of interest and technology to
take a microscopic look at the teaching process as well as
the macroscopic view. There is much to commend in the
study of small parts of the whole experience, in addition
to looking for the long-term trends. Comparative studies
are now more easily carried out because of equipment to
record various techniques and then study them at leisure.

The consequence of a learning experience should be
looked at in terms of the development of the whole man.
For one student an experience in the class may be the only
one in his background while for another it may be a
familiar part. The amount of irrelevance in many of the
prescribed programs in higher education might over-
whelm all of us. It does seem important to ask if the learning experience and its consequences are of much use in
the development of the whole man. A student of Chinese
culture might be in a general studies course in which the
Chinese culture is being studied and be able to contribute
to the class more than he receives. He may experience a
different kind of consequence, that of being able to be of
use. To his development as a whole man, this may be a
very important part of his self-esteem. Within the class
there are those who by superior ability or earlier attainment can be helpers to classmates while others from the
class must lean upon helpers to make it through.

In summary, the output or consequences of the learning experience represent a dimension whose parameters

are not well known. It is too easy to say that knowledge, skills, or even attitudes are the intended purpose. It is too trite to say that these outputs are uniform for all members of the class or meet the same needs for all members. With the rich variety of differences in members of a group who are involved in a common instructional process, the outcomes need be thought of in as complex terms as each individual's need, as well as the commonality of the announced purpose of the course.

patterns of learning experiences

typical patterns

THE few studies in the field of patterns of learning experiences for groups show that the space envelope is most often a classroom and the method most often the lecture. It involves a single teacher with a score of students joined together in the common enterprise for approximately an hour's time. This experience tends to be repeated several times during the week for the total of fifteen to twenty-four periods constitutiong a quarter or semester. Students take notes, discuss, recite, and occasionally take short quizzes. It is of interest to know why this has become the typical pattern, outranking tutorials and self-instruction.

Just as this is the classical pattern and has persisted for many generations, there is an emerging pattern. It is a functional one. The student not only selects an institution and courses in it that reflect his interests and needs, he also works actively to change the environment he has selected. This collective effort, often the adversary tech-

nique, is effective. More change occurred in college cur-
riculums in 1969 because of student pressures than for any
other reason. If this does become the pattern for change,
it may cause concern. Not all of the goals the majority
champion are for the best intellectual life. The emerging
pattern is likely, however, to be quite relevant.

atypical patterns

As the opposite of the typical pattern, the atypical pattern
is also worth review. Sometimes these patterns are developed simply for the shock value they contain, but often
they are honest experiments by people trying to find
unique ways of accomplishing a purpose. Occasionally it
is tied to the psychological needs of the leader. The teacher
who tells a class that he will leave the decision as to what
they learn entirely up to them uses a shock procedure but
it has at times led to thoughtful reinspection of what the
class is for. Having the class itself take on part of the teaching process is another variation. Carrying out the class assignments in entirely different surroundings than the classroom, say in a ghetto area or on board a ship, would be
still another. Several publications reported in the bibliography describe these innovative procedures. A number of
new colleges and several junior colleges have dared to
break traditional patterns of class groups by use of non-
class continuous learning. Some use a common pool of resources instead of classrooms.

It is interesting to explore the extreme locations along
the matrix and to contemplate the consequences of using
these extremes. It should be recognized that for several
points on the matrix there is no way to accomplish these

extremes in terms of present technology and nor can one find reasons for using them. But many new ventures are now possible. Take for example the desire that might occur at some time to have one student taught by many teachers in one session. This may be the case of a doctoral candidate who deserves the time of five full professors as he may be in the finishing stages of his original work expressed in his thesis. But could one hundred be assembled? This did occur when Colonel Frank Borman was given a team of one hundred educators, psychologists, and medical men to brief him upon space travel, its loneliness, its effect upon physiological functions. For two days one hundred assembled experts briefed this one student. When multimillions of dollars are spent upon this one venture, this drawing together of live talent may seem desirable. Technology makes it now possible for a dozen physicians to confer on one patient. One might also ask questions concerning the ability of students to teach fellow students when no real difference in ability or experience exists between those leading and those following. One may also ask about the ability of the mind to receive several streams of sensory information simultaneously without undue interference. These are just a few of the many explorations that could be made to the edge of present practice along the grid.

emerging patterns

The trend through the sixties has been to more open discussion in class and many bypass techniques. Free schools parallel credit courses. Institutes parallel departments, and students now learn on their own or use instructors. The flexibility and the variety of experiences might in itself be called an emerging pattern. In still another sense the purpose of all this activity is to lead the learner to a given outcome in the most effective fashion. Review of ways to do this now show that some methods work better than others. It also shows that people vary as to which method they prefer. Fitting then the best academic learning situation to the individual seems to be the name of the game in the seventies. Much will be done in common with the help of media for huge numbers. More books in the library can be made available to the individuals at his own time and his own rate. The same subject content will soon be available in verbal and nonverbal form. We might say this is a day when people are able to afford the luxury of not only two cars but dual methods of instruction as well.

Not a few people express alarm about the direction learning is going. There are those who see our present system passing on to complete automation and, concerned about their ability to influence it, lock in upon protective standards at this time. Such standards include assurance that they will not teach more than a given number of contact hours per week, or that certain increments in salary will be guaranteed to all in the program. This is not to decry the rightful demands of the teachers union, but at the same time not let unreasoned demands block the experimental processes in higher education. Recent institutional efforts, in response to student unrest, to slam the door upon those who resist authority could postpone the showdown on the real struggle which is between the student and the faculty member. There is need for substantial change in the way higher education is conducted. This will take place sooner if freedom to criticize and respect for orderly procedure survive. Perhaps a struggle within the university at the present time is wholesome, and no good trend will develop unless these stirrings are deep enough to cause so large an amount of ferment.

literature
of the sixties

DURING the sixties the literature relating technology to higher education is best characterized by its increasing quantity in the last half of this decade. Not only has the flow increased, so also has the complexity of ideas expressed. There are more ideas for systems, and a greater number of controlled experiments reported. Most of the hardware was known during this decade. The more recent attention is to application, longitudinal studies, and the inevitable software and brainware. Although films and television play a large part in the literature and the concern for space is ever more evident, the largest concern now seems to be the utilization of the computer.

For the last few years more than a thousand articles and books per year have been published. This is up from a fourth that amount at the beginning of the sixties. The main sources for these publications are universities and public schools, particularly from the fields of psychology, audiovisual, and education. Next are government agencies contributing not only to research but to reports of prac-

tical applications. Industry, the major producer of the
hardware, is less well represented in the literature; however, its influence is growing as many manufacturers link
up with publishers for a more marketable product. In
general it seems that each person is doing his own thing
with scanty wide-scale distribution of findings.

The distribution of the literature among the seven categories of the matrix and the kinds of articles most evident
may be grouped as follows:

topics	kind of article
PROCESS	Methods and Innovations
PERSONS	Students, Teacher
ENCLOSURES	Architecture, Functional Design, Construction Materials
OUTPUTS	Outcomes, Tests, Statements of Goals
TRANSFERENCES	Feedback Techniques
INPUTS	Measurement, Categories, Group Concepts
TIME	Intermixed Time Modes, Special Relationships

It must be admitted that much shaping went into the inclusion of articles in the bibliography. Theoretical works
were not emphasized, and the technologies used in pre-
college programs were largely ignored. There are a few
antitechnology articles describing, for example, how technology perpetuates an allegedly archaic system, namely the
lecture, by making it possible to amplify the teacher's
voice and image for larger groups. As a general observation, it would appear that the flow of literature now ex-
ceeds in several categories the good works that might come

from it. Most writers are reporting small-scale experiments
or expounding theories.

Instead of an annotated bibliography fifteen categories
have been selected, and in each some of the literature is
described. There follows an alphabetical listing of selected
titles from the decade of the sixties. After each entry in
parentheses is the number of the category which in this
writer's judgment the book or article was best located.

1
philosophies related to technology and higher education

A number of authors have set their hand to describing
in broad general terms the nature and substance of technology and higher education. Most often the comments
turn critical. Partly because it relates what is happening
to larger social issues and to the goals of man, it may be
the most enduring of the observations made about higher
education. It may also be the most varied in points of view.
To illustrate this point a sampling of the literature of the
sixties is further categorized.

There is a group of sharp critics of the topic. Miasma,
darkness, torpidity, end of a grand tradition, and the diagnosis of failure are ascriptions applied by authors such as
Snow, Rickover, Shrag, and Hooper. On the more opti-
mistic side are aphorisms such as the silent conquest by
Michael and learning for mastery in an article by Bloom.
It is perhaps characteristic of our age that more critics
than proponents have appeared. It is only fair to add that
these general treatments of the subject are for the most
part well-balanced philosophical statements and speak
more to the dual possibilities of technology for much
harm or good.

Two other aspects emerge in the literature. One is the

look to the future. Those who give it perspective are Randall, Eurich, and persons like Walker who speak of the next hundred years, and McLuhan who pictures media as the new extension of man. The second aspect is from authors who address the matter of shaping higher education by media and technology. Zajack suggests shaping can be like an hourglass or a funnel. Morse sees it as management change; Mager would prepare instructional objectives; and Bruner calls it "process" education. Ostar and Burke are most concerned about the relationships with other institutions and human values.

In spite of the rapid pace of change there has been time for a sizeable number of thoughful writers to place what is happening in larger perspective. If technology does make substantial and permanent change in higher education, it will not have been done without the advice and counsel of several scores of writers who have put their works before the public.

2. systems analysis and summaries

Another broad category in which articles are grouped is the cluster of analytic and design-oriented studies which tend to summarize the whole field. Their emphasis is more on analysis than synthesis as was the case of the previous category. It includes the bibliographies, annotated and plain.

Among the bibliographies are those of Hickey on computer-assisted instruction, Fry on teaching machines, Finn on new media, and the works of others compiling information on such things as films, television, and instructional methods. In all, there are a few dozen summary-type works, some of which group the literature into categories. Caldwell's two volume annotated bibliography lists eight thousand entries of the last twenty years arranged in twelve chapter sections. Section four on the nature of the impact of science and technology contains the most relevant references to the discussion here. Not to be overlooked are the recent surveys of the literature by the Department of Higher Education of the United States Office of Education.

Related to the summaries of bibliographies are the statements of strategy and system design itself. Men such as Watson, Ott, Koch, and Kaufmann suggest strategies including management techniques, classification of decision-making situations, model building, and tool making. In terms of design Tanner, Mauch, and Barson consider general design, Goss emphasizes acquisition schemes, Freedman suggests communications, Silvern looks to cybernetics, and Au chooses the heuristic approach. The cautions in systems design suggested by Vidale are of more than passing interest. Root provides a modest preview to the field.

It is apparent from the literature that systems design came of age in the sixties and now takes its place in the concept of higher education. It is an enterprise to be managed and made accountable. It is clear that these experts view higher education to be no different than other large operations that can be analyzed and considered as a system. This concept facilitates the plug-in features of technology. The inputs, outputs, functions and components are considered sufficiently well understood to be manipulated by analysis, quantitative techniques, model building, and the like. In the seventies it is likely that this test of replaceability of many of the teacher's former functions will be made. Most of the systems analysts feel confident a better operation will result.

3. *theories—both special and general*

A significant portion of the literature can be grouped around the theories concerning evaluation, process, and perception, both general and multisensory. From the fields of psychology in particular and the social sciences in general, the situation of the educator has been illuminated by the works of those approaching learning from the standpoint of the individual. At one end of this broad range is Hockberg with his theory of perception. At the other is Benjamin Bloom with his taxonomy of educational objectives. Most of the literature selected for inclusion stresses evaluation and process. Because of the author's special interest in the new possibilities of learning inherent in multiple sensory perception, this too is included.

Evaluations both in breadth and depth now occur frequently in higher education. In the fifties and sixties educational television was carefully evaluated. Few theories came from it. The works of Standlee and Popham suggest that the use of quizzes improved achievement early in a course. McKeechie, Pryluck, and Osgood have taken on the classroom, the cinema, and measurement of meaning respectively. Theories are now emerging. Greissman uses educational models to develop theories. The volume of evaluation studies has expanded greatly in this decade. The hypotheses of these studies should bear fruit in the seventies in the formation of additional theories.

Process is now receiving serious consideration by a number of writers. Shoemaker, Follettie, and Worth see meaningful relationships in the sequencing and organization of topics. Terrace has a theory about error-free learning. It is interesting to compare his ideas with those of Suedfeld on the search procedure in learning. Severin talks about cues, and Sebeok about the codes in signaling. Cook is interested in the intervention of prompting. Kretch represents a growing number who write on the chemistry of learning. Process as an important aspect of learning is having a field day with the theorists, and it is likely to continue.

Of special interest to the author are the problems and possibilities in multisensory aspects of learning. This seems so closely related to the resources that technology is now ready to make available that the readiness of man to embrace these becomes of major importance. Neumann has a general article on verbal vs. nonverbal methods in learning. Severin represents a group looking at multiple channel communication. Van Mondfrans and Travers are concerned about redundancy while Kaska is trying to construct the concept of multiple reality. Hartman, Harcleroad, and Neisser all share a concern for this essential sorting process and overarching meaning that multiple sensory information require.

4. *media in general related to higher education*

A relatively small number of books and articles have been written on the general topic of media. Most of these such as Ely refer to the audiovisual process. Lumsdaine refers to instruments as distinct from the media. Some, such as David, refer to specific devices, namely the computer, the television, and the telephone. Mild and Doughty refer to the media as a system, while Wedemeyer thinks of it as a tool. What is evident from all of this is that the various skills and techniques are now being thought of in a comprehensive framework. The interrelationships are not fully understood, but most agree with McLuhan that saturation is upon us. To my mind there is need for more thoughtful articles on the overview of media, particularly by teams of social scientists, behavioral psychologists, and the men who know the hardware.

5. *the media center*

The aspiration of many campuses is for a media center which will enhance the learning process and not upset too much the accustomed tasks of the classroom and the teacher. An essential question then is who is to do it. If experts are obtained, the faculty often feels removed, and the center may become a bureaucracy. If the faculty takes it on, it is usually at the expense of other tasks already taxing. The literature for the most part holds out the dream that a media center is a fine thing. Media centers at private liberal arts colleges are often featured. Oklahoma Christian College and Florida Atlantic College are examples. Many larger universities have such centers, for example, University of California at Irvine, Miami University, Southern Illinois University, and Michigan State University. Some emphasize one feature, such as computer-assisted instruction used at Amherst College, and many larger institutions have the media centers attached to a particular department, such as Education at Wisconsin and Audiovisual at Syracuse.

A growing body of literature considers the media center as an entity. Wyman asks the question whose empire it is. Margolis gives guidelines for support and Barnes ideas for organization and administration. Symposia for discussion of media centers are frequent. The most rapidly growing front for these centers is the community college. Martinson's article is typical of this development.

There is much that is yet amorphous about the extensive use of media on the college campus. Here again is an area about which more should be written lest our practice be the contagion of wide-eyed enthusiasm.

6. *programming*

Largest in terms of number of publications is the category including efforts at automation, programmed instruction, teaching machines, self-instruction, and managing the individual in the classroom. This is the area of greatest upheaval and fresh starts. One gets the impression everyone is doing his own thing. There are fewer coordinative efforts and less bibliographies. It may stem from the fact that the field is one of proprietary interests. The frequent mergers of equipment manufacturers and book publishers also give rise to a flurry of matings of authors and techniques. In many ways it is one of the most exciting fields because it represents the redirected energy of the teacher who for so long has been the individual classroom star.

Articles by Hatfield on strategy and Ofiesh on trends represent the scanty group on overview. Many have written on the management of the individual, as has Weisgerber, but few have taken on the programmed instruction of groups or the handicapped, as has Pfau. Many have also written on special topics such as costs, efficiency, effectiveness, branching concepts, and an endless stream of programs. There are occasional handbooks such as the one by Cox. If there be a missionary movement in higher education today, it is the gospel of programming with intellectuals, mercenaries, and devotees ready to help.

7. computer relations

The fast rise of the computer in contemporary society did not bypass the university. In many ways it is its original home, although the cost and complexity of its operation have directed it to banks and industries faster than to smaller colleges. The computer is the one technological tool that has outdone the telephone in becoming ubiquitous. With this broad base it has been possible to try it out in the classroom for fast feedback techniques and for individualization of instruction by computer-aided instruction. Next to programming it is the most prolific field.

Tracing the literature from the general to the specific, Hamblen has made a general appraisal of the use of computers in higher education but more in terms of funds and research than of the classroom. Ramo pointed out its advantages as an intellectual tool. Suppes for Stanford University and Holtzman for University of Texas represent the spokesmen for campus-wide efforts. There are many articles about courses from exotic languages to piloting planes. Waddor talks about labs, Kerr about math, and Jernigan about the library. If the prediction is true that only about 6 percent of the higher education effort of instruction will be given over to the computer by 1975, a tremendous impact has already been felt. The equipment has come faster than the assimilation of computer languages and so-called software. And these are both ahead of the training of users to manage on their own. It may take a decade to both persuade and involve the faculty. By then access to a console should be about as easy as dialing long distance—or nearly so.

8. *educational television*

The highwater mark in the literature on closed-circuit and educational television came early in the decade of the sixties. It was experiencing some of the same appeal that the computer enjoyed; that it would make a dramatic breakthrough. Broadcast television is on many university campuses as a public service and training program for TV majors. Closed circuit programming is available on more campuses, particularly new community colleges. Mini or micro use of television is now popular in education, sales, and home economics programs. It makes one wonder if literature volume rises when funds from foundations and the federal government are pumped into a new field. Happily the trend has been set, and most college students will get at least a small portion of their undergraduate instruction by television in the seventies. Along with the rise of television has been the greater use of film. These topics were joined in this category as an important visual emphasis.

The literature is abundant with respect to state systems such as Colorado, Texas, New York, and California. Regional networks have had irregular success such as the Midwest Airborne Television Network. After the heroic efforts by the Ford Foundation to provide evidence that television instruction can be as effective as that of a live teacher in a class situation, the concern has shifted to attitudes of permissiveness while watching by Woodward, hostility of faculty by Evans, Smith, and Colville, and the administrative problems by Erickson. The new interest in quick feedback information in a skill course such as golf or a practice teaching assignment that a portable television camera can give has brought the art of television to the do-it-yourself level.

9. simulation and modeling

The technique of simulation has been made possible by the computer and could be rightly placed beneath it. As a special technique and one that is rapidly growing in popularity, it may be important to identify it for the next decade. Gaming as described by Boocock and simulated laboratory for nurses as described by Bitzer represent the new front. Verduin has devised conceptual models in teacher education. More frequently it is used in large-scale problems where time is saved by making a model or stripping down a problem to look at its parts, arrest its progress, or just to try it over again. Hodgson has tried it at the Industrial College of the Armed Forces as a computer simulation of international relations. Curricula, career parameters, and decision making are now being considered.

10. feedback, retrieval, and outputs

The literature now contains examples of feedback aided by technology. Various class formations used by Siegal provided different levels of feedback. It was augmented further by a computer connection for quick processing of class data from quizzes and opinionaires. Salomon used pre and posttest reactions to self-viewing one's teaching performance on videotape. Almstead avers that there is not enough talkback. Woodward has examined the effects of immediate feedback. These examples of the literature indicate that the field is being explored but not yet systematically. In the author's opinion there is much to be gained from a more thorough exploration of the avenues by which the junior and senior learners can be brought more into a maximum utilization balance. The new tools of technology will make this area more accessible than before.

11. innovations and creativity

A cursory look at the literature on innovation in general reveals that technology has made its imprint on innovation. It has long been known that invention is related to economic growth, and innovations in education seem to be related to technological breakthroughs. Apparently the dimensions of change as discussed by Scanlon and Hamlin take into account the visual revolution and the computer. Taylor and Williams relate instructional media and creativity. Blank describes a league for experimentation and innovation. The diffusion of innovation as described by Rogers leaves place for the inventor and the technician. It must be admitted that innovation and creativity are still products thought to be purely mental; however, technology can bring faster interchanges of information and more rapid opportunity to change one's premises. Evans and Leppmann describe the resistance to innovation in higher education based largely on television studies. Caterino describes how student involvement in making media materials provides an opportunity for innovation. The new media provide the pathways. The adventuresome ones will explore the pathways. In this category of the literature optimism seems unbridled and the decade of the seventies most promising.

12. *vocational and professional relationships*

A category was provided for the expected comments in the literature on the impact of technology on the college training for these vocations and professions. Relatively little was found. Bern describes the need for educational engineers. An American Association of Colleges for Teacher Education project called Professional Teacher Education—A Program Design hints at programming but little technology. Gale in his article, "No Room for Amateurs," describes the audiovisual profession as one requiring expertise. Apparently the only people seriously concerned about technology's impact upon their vocational future are the media specialists themselves as in an article by Erickson and another by Larson. Evans apparently sees some concerns ahead in his article, "Higher Education and Unemployment—Some Paradoxes." It is the author's observation that the paucity of literature on the technological aspects of vocational preparation has led industry to train its own people with the technologies it will use. There is a certain ambiguity at this point as to the adequacy of collegiate instruction with media and the way it is done in industry and government. For example, should undergraduate students studying accounting be familiar with the computer much like the one they will be using with a business or industry? Or should a computer language be known and used? These and other questions cloud the issue for university administrators; however, there is little help yet from the literature on this subject.

13. special programs and applications

One of the richest sources of literature on technology and higher education is in the area of special projects. Although the representation in this bibliography is limited, by far the largest portion of the general literature is represented by the specific applications. The items included here are arbitrary and might have been placed under "Programming" or "Research." They do represent the rapidly increasing resource of specific practices and situations. No one has yet put this together in a composite whole; however, if it is done, it will provide a necessary liaison between fields and the basis for further study and application. The topics run the range from a multimedia kit program to the efforts to provide interaction with individual differences by the methods of presenting program instructional materials. The abundance of articles reflects the use of a particular media with many on the matter of tape retrieval, terminal use, films, and television.

14. the space envelope

The environment within which the learning experience occurs is as broad as the community and the world on one hand and as small as the classroom and the student's mind on the other. The literature is just as dispersed. Antioch College tells of its undergraduate experience abroad. Milton gives objective data after learning without class attendance, and Sharp speaks of architectural steps in facility planning. In fact, McIntyre, Haney, Mattox, Jamrich, and a host of others describe the facilities development through technology's assistance. In general, space has been accepted as one of the important aspects of learning, and the number of articles is growing. It still represents a small slice of the literature, but more should develop in the seventies.

15. *the teacher as a person*

This category was reserved for articles dealing with the person in the learning process and also the teacher. Happily the human element has not been overlooked, and the literature is abundant. Most of it is pointed to the person as the recipient of technology's thrust. Seldom is he thought to be the driver of the car. This exception does occur with Mahaffy's article on expanding limited lives with media and Ingraham's on new strategies and roles for the social studies teacher. There is also an article by Fisher on the teacher's growing role. If any observation can be made over the sixties concerning the relative role of the teacher and the machine, it seems that toward the end of that decade to be a more equal struggle. I look forward in the seventies for the literature to reveal that man has mastered the machine in the classroom and uses it as easily as the typewriter and the telephone.

In summary then, as the number of participants using technology has grown, a fairly constant percentage of those involved write about it. With more expected to enter these relationships in the seventies, the literature is likely to grow still more. The purpose of this small volume is to identify the parameters for learning on seven different scales and to observe the present location of these constants and how they might change. It is likely that technology will make a permanent impact on higher education and change some long-established constants whether it be the student-teacher ratio or the learning rate. Visual materials, electronic message handling devices open up new relationships, some of which will be quickly accepted and others resisted. The voice of the student in his own self-determination is stronger than it has been since medieval times and his influence will be increasingly felt. The literature is both record and prologue. The reader must determine for himself which part forecasts the future.

bibliography/index

key to bibliography

Abel, Frederick Paul. "Use of Closed Circuit Television in Teacher Education: Relationship to Achievement and Subject Matter Understanding." Ph.D. dissertation, University of Minnesota, 1960. **8**

Abelson, Philip H. "Computer-Assisted Instruction," *Science* 162, November 1968, p. 855. **7**

Abrams, Irwin, and Arnold, David B. "The American College and International Education." New Dimensions in Higher Education, no. 27. Durham, N. C.: Duke University, 1967. **14**

Ackoff, Russell L., ed. *Progress in Operations Research.* Vol. 1. New York: John Wiley and Sons, 1969. **3**

Adams, Jack A. "Response, Feedback, and Learning." *Psychological Bulletin* 70 (1968) : 486–504. **10**

Adams, Walter, and John A. Garraty. *Is the World Our Campus?* East Lansing: Michigan State University Press, 1960. **14**

Allen, Dwight W.; Fortune, Jimmie C.; and Cooper, James M. "The Stanford Summer Micro-Teaching Clinic, 1965." *Journal of Teacher Education* 18 (1967) : 389–93. **15**

Allen, Dwight W., and Bushnell, Don D. *The Computer in American Education.* New York: John Wiley and Sons, 1967. **7**

Allen, William H. "Television for California Schools." *Bulletin of the California State Department of Education,* 39, April 1960, 48 pp. **8**

————. "Audio Visual Communication." In *Encyclopedia of Educational Research.* 3d ed. Edited by C. W. Harms. New York: Macmillan Co., 1960. **4**

Almstead, F. E., and Graf, R. W. "Talkback: The Missing Ingredient." *Audiovisual Instruction,* vol. 5, no. 4, April 1960, pp. 110–12. **10**

Alspaugh, J. W. "Utilization of Computing and Data Processing in Education." *Clearing House* 43 (1969) : 544–47. **12**

Anderson, Richard C.; Faust, Gerald W.; and Roderick, Marianne C. "Overprompting in Programmed Instruction." *Journal of Educational Psychology* 49 (1968) : 88–93. **10**

Andreyeu, N. D. "Models as a Tool in the Development of Linguisitic Theory." *Word* 18, April–August 1962, pp. 186–97. **9**

Atkinson, Richard C. "The Computer is a Tutor." *Psychology Today* 1 (1968) : 36–39, 57–59. **7**

Arnsdorf, Val. "Teaching Social Studies with Map-Overlays." California *Journal of Educational Research* 16 (1965) : 65–74. **8**

Au, Tung. "Heuristic Approach to Systems Design." *Journal of Engineering Education* 49, March 1969, pp. 861–65. **2**

Audio Visual Communication Review. Vol. 16, no. 2. Summer 1968. **4**

Audio Visual Communication Review. Vol. 17, no. 1. Spring 1969. **4**

Axford, Roger W. "College-Community Consultation." Ph.D. dissertation, Northern Illinois University, 1967. **14**

Baloff, Nicholas, and Becker, Selwyn W. "A Model of Group Adaption to Problem-Solving Tasks." *Organizational Behavior and Human Performance* 3 (1968) : 217–38. **9**

Barabasz, Arreed F. "A Study of Recall and Retention of Accelerated Lecture Presentation." *Journal of Communication* 18 (1968) : 283–87. **10**

Barlow, John A. "Note: Student Cheating in Studying Programmed Material." *Psychological Record* 17 (1967) : 515–16. **15**

————. "Conversation Chaining in Teaching Machine Programs." *Psychological Reports* 7 (1960) : 187–93. **6**

Barnes, Virginia C. "The Organization and Administration of the Instructional Materials Center in Medium-Sized School Districts." *Dissertation Abstracts,* vol. 21, pp. 1104–5. Ann Arbor, Mich.: University Microfilms, 1960. **5**

Barrington, H. "A Survey of Instructional Television Researches." *Educational Research* 8 (1965) : 8–25. **2**

Barson, J., and Heinich, R. "The Systems Approach to Instruction." DAVI 1966 Convention, San Diego (audiotape). Boulder: National Tape Repository, University of Colorado. **2**

Barson, John, dir. "Instructional Systems Development: A Demonstration and Evaluation Project." East Lansing: Michigan State University, 1967. **2**

Baskin, Samuel et al. Innovation in Higher Education—Developments, Research, and Priorities. New Dimensions in Higher Education, no. 19. Durham, N. C.: Duke University, 1967. **11**

Bauldree, Aaron N. "Individual and Group Differences in Learning Under Two Different Modes of Computer Assisted Instruction." Ph.D. dissertation, Florida State University, 1968. **7**

Bergen, Jane et al. *Robots in the Classroom.* Jericho, N. Y.: Exposition Press, 1965. **6**

Berman, Mark L. "Educational Innovation from College Down." *Educational Technology,* January 1969, pp. 31–32. **11**

————. "Shaping Performance on Programmed Materials." *Psychological Reports* 31 (1967) : 29–32. **6**

Bern, H. A. "Wanted: Educational Engineers." *Phi Delta Kappan* 48 (1967) : 230–36. **12**

Bernardis, Amo De; Crossman, David M.; and Miller, Thomas E. "Media, Technology, and IMC Space Requirements." *Audiovisual Instruction*, February 1965, pp. 107–13. **4**

Bertalanffy, Ludwig Von. *Organismic Psychology and Systems Theory.* Worcester, Mass.: Clark University Press, 1966. **2**

A Bibliography of Educational Television and Related Communication Systems. National Association of Educational Broadcasters, July 1967. **8**

Bitzer, Donald L. "*Plato: An Electronic Teaching Device.*" Paper presented at the annual meeting of the American Society for Engineering Education in Philadelphia, June 1963. **13**

Bitzer, Donald L., and Braunfeld, Peter G. "Description and Use of a Computer Controlled Teaching System." Proceedings of the National Electronics Conference, October 1962. **7**

Bitzer, Donald L.; Hicks, Bruce L.; Johnson, Roger L.; and Lyman, Elisabeth R. "The Plato System: Current Research and Development." *Institute of Electrical Engineering Education Transactions on Human Factors in Electronics,* vol. HFE–8, no. 2, June 1967, pp. 64–70. **7**

Bitzer, Donald L.; Lyman, E. R.; and Suchman, J. R. *A Study in Scientific Inquiry Using the Plato System.* Coordinated Science Laboratory Report R-260. Urbana: University of Illinois, December 1965. **7**

Bitzer, Donald L., and Slottow, H. G. "The Plasma Display Panel— A Digitally Addressable Display with Inherent Memory." In *Proceedings Fall Joint Computer Conference 1966,* pp. 541–47. Urbana: University of Illinois, 1966. **13**

Biveres, Lyle W. "Feedback Complexity and Self Direction in Programmed Instruction." *Psychological Reports,* 14 (1964) : 155–60. **10**

Bjerstedt, Ake. "Mapping the Effect-Structure of Didactic Sequences." *Didakometry* 2 (1964) : 11. **10**

————. "A Simulator-Test Approach to the Study of Teachers' Interaction Tendencies." *Educational and Psychological Interactions* 29 (1968) : p. 21. **9**

Black, Hillel. "Automation Still in Future." *New York Times,* 12 January 1968, p. 74. **6**

Blane, Linda Marlin. *The Relationship of the Number of Hours of Television Instruction to Student Attitudes.* Report 12, University of Miami, January 1965. **11**

Blank, Stanley S. "Teaching Machines: What Have Studies In the Classroom Shown?" *California Journal of Educational Research* 12 (1961) : 99–115. **6**

Blick, Kenneth A., and McClurkin, John I. "The Effect of Stimulus Characteristics on Immediate and Delayed Transposition." *Psychonomic Science* 13 (1968) : 233–34. **10**

Bloom, Benjamin S. *Stability and Change in Human Characteristics.* New York: John Wiley and Sons, 1964. **1**

———. "Learning for Mastery." *Administrators Notebook,* vol. 16, no. 8. Chicago: Midwest Administration Center, University of Chicago, April, 1968. **1**

Bloom, Benjamin S., ed. *Taxonomy of Educational Objectives: The Classification of Educational Goals: Handbook I: Cognitive Domain.* New York: Longmans, Green, and Company, 1956. **3**

"The Board Reports," Illinois Board of Higher Education, vol. 1, no. 2, Spring 1968. **14**

Bobren, Howard M. "Student Attitudes Toward Instructional Television: Additional Evidence." *Audio Visual Communication Review* 8 (1960) : 281–83. **8**

Boersma, Frederick J. "Effects of Delay of Information Feedback and Length of Postfeedback Interval on Linear Programmed Learning." *Journal of Educational Psychology* 57 (1966) : 140–45. **10**

Bond, Jack H. *Using Simulation Techniques to Change Attitudes of Education Majors Toward Professional Course Objectives.* Monmouth: Teaching Research Division, Oregon State System of Higher Education, 1965. **9**

Boocock, Sarane S. "The Effects of Games with Simulated Environments Upon Student Learning." *Dissertation Abstracts A,* vol. 27, p. 3127. Ann Arbor, Mich.: University Microfilms, 1967. **9**

———. "The Life Career Game." *Personnel and Guidance Journal* 46 (1967) : 328–34. **9**

———. "Simulation Games Today—III." *Educational Technology,* vol. 9, no. 2, February 1969, pp. 14–15. **9**

Borko, Harold, ed. *Computer Applications in the Behavioral Sciences.* Englewood Cliffs, N. J.: Prentice-Hall, 1962. **7**

Bowers, Norman D. "Meaningful Learning and Retention: Task and Method Variables," *Review of Educational Research* 31, December 1961, pp. 522–34. **3**

Braam, Leonard S., and Berger, Allen. "Effectiveness of Four Methods of Increasing Reading Rate, Comprehension, and Flexibility." *Journal of Reading* 11 (1968) : 346–52. **13**

Brethower, Dale M. *Programmed Instruction and Programming Techniques—The Analysis of an Educational Technology.* Ann Arbor, Mich.: The Institute for Behavioral Research and Programmed Instruction, 1962. **6**

Brickman, William H., and Stanley Lehrer, eds. *Automation, Education and Human Values.* New York: School and Society Books, Division of Society for the Advancement of Education, 1966. **1**

Brinkmann, Erwin H. "Educability in Visualization of Objects in Space: A Programmed Instruction Approach." Ph.D. dissertation, University of Michigan, 1963. **13**

Broyles, Glenwood E. "Learning Models for Television: Improving the Program Content." *Audiovisual Instruction* 12 (1967) : 917–20. **8**

Brown, George W.; Miller, James G.; and Keenan, Thomas A., authors and editors. *EDUNET: Report of the Educon Summer Study on Information Networks.* New York: John Wiley and Sons, 1967. **5**

Brown, James W., and Thornton, James W., Jr. *New Media in Higher Education.* Washington: Association for Higher Education and the Division of Audiovisual Instructional Service of the National Education Association, 1963. **4**

Brown, James W., and Norberg, Kenneth D. *Administering Educational Media.* New York: McGraw-Hill Book Company, 1965. **5**

Brown, Louis H. "Retrieving Media Information According to Content or Subject Area," *Audiovisual Instruction,* February 1969, pp. 71–74. **10**

Brumbaugh, Donald. "Higher Education," *Audiovisual Instruction* 14, June–July 1969, pp. 75–76. **1**

Bruner, Jerome S. "The Course of Cognitive Growth." *American Psychologist* (1964) : 1–15. **3**

———. *The Process of Education.* Cambridge, Mass.: Harvard University Press, 1961. **1**

Bugliarello, George. "Developing Creativity in an Engineering Science Course—Socrates Revisited." *Journal of Engineering Education,* vol. 59, no. 7, March 1969, pp. 877–80. **11**

Bullock, Donald H. "Comments on Oakes' 'Use of Teaching Machines as a Study Aid in an Introductory Psychology Course'," *Psychological Report,* 8, February 1961, p. 96. **6**

Burke, John G., ed. *The New Technology and Human Values.* Belmont, Calif.: Wadsworth Publishing Company, 1966. **1**

Burns, Richard W. "Suggestions for Involving Teachers in Innovation," *Educational Technology,* January 1969, pp. 27–28. **11**

Bushnell, Don D., ed. *Computer in American Education.* New York: John Wiley and Sons, 1968. **7**

———. *The Automation of School Information Systems: Monograph no. 1.* Washington: Department of Audiovisual Instruction, National Education Association, 1964. **7**

———. "The Role of the Computer in Future Instructional Systems." *Audio Visual Communication Review* 11, March–April 1963. **7**

———. "Computer-Based Teaching Machines." *Journal of Educational Research* 55, June–July 1962, pp. 528–31. **7**

Bushnell, Don D., and Borko, Harold. *Information Retrieval Systems and Education.* Santa Monica, Calif.: System Development Corporation, September, 1962. **2**

Caldwell, Lynton K., ed. *Science Technology and Public Policy, A Selected and Annotated Bibliography,* vol. 1 and 2, Bloomington, Ind.: Indiana University, 1968. **2**

Cameron, Charles C. "Five Schools Linked Together for TV Teaching." *Journal Medical Education* 34 (1959) : 1077–81. **8**

Campeau, Peggy L. "Test Anxiety and Feedback in Programmed Instruction." *Journal of Educational Psychology* 59 (1968) : 159–63. **10**

Cardozier, V. R. ed. *Teacher Education in Agriculture.* Danville, Ill.: Interstate Printers and Publishers, 1967. **12**

Carnegie Corporation of New York Quarterly. Vol. 13, no. 4, October 1965. **4**

Caro, Paul W., Jr. "The Effect of Class Attendance and 'Time Structured' Content on Achievement in General Psychology." *Journal of Educational Psychology* 53, April 1962, pp. 76–80. **14**

Carpenter, C. R., and Greenhill, L. P. *An Investigation of Closed-Circuit Television for Teaching University Courses: Instructional Television Research: Report Number Two.* University Park: Pennsylvania State University, 1958. **8**

Carpenter, Finley. *Teaching Machines and Programmed Instruction.* Syracuse: The Library of Education, Center for Applied Research in Education, 1963. **6**

Casey, John P. *School Ability and the Problem Solving Process: Studies of the Problem Solving Processes of Gifted and Average Children.* Carbondale: Southern Illinois University Foundation, 1967. **1**

Caterino, S. J. "Student Involvement In Making Visual Perception Materials." *Audiovisual Instruction,* November 1969, pp. 74–75. **11**

Chansky, Norman M. "Learning: A Function of Schedule and Type of Feedback." *Psychology Report* 7, October 1960, p. 362. **10**

Charp, Sylvia. "A Computer-Assisted Instruction System." *Audiovisual Instruction* 14, March 1969, pp. 61–64. **7**

Christian, R. W. "Guides to Programmed Learning." *Harvard Business Review* 6 (1962) : 36–44, 173–179. **6**

Chu, G. C., and Schramm, W. *Learning from Television: What the Research Says.* Stanford, Calif.: Institution for Communication Research, 1967. **8**

Clark, Philip M. "A Model for Individual Differences in Modes of Processing Information." Ph.D. dissertation, University of Michigan, 1967. **9**

Clarke, Wentworth. "Simulation for Stimulation." *Audiovisual Instruction* 14, April 1969, pp. 44–48. **9**

Cobin, Martin T., and Clevenger, Theodore, Jr. "Television Instruction Course Content, and Teaching Experience Level: An Experimental Study in the Basic Course in Oral Interpretation." *Speech Monogram* 28 (1961) : 16–20. **8**

Cochran, Lida M. "Four Significant Media Projects of 1967–1968," *Audiovisual Instruction* 13, June–July 1968, pp. 578–83. **13**

Cogswell, John F. *Analysis of Instructional Systems.* Santa Monica, Calif.: Systems Development Corporation TM-1493/201/00, 1966. **2**

Cogswell, John F.; Egbert, Robert L.; Marsh, Donald G.; and Yett, Frank A. *Purpose and Strategy of the School Simulation Project.* Santa Monica, Calif.: Systems Development Corporation, December, 1963. **9**

Cohen, Gillian. "The Effect of Codability of the Stimulus on Recognition Reaction Times." *British Journal of Psychology* 60 (1969) : 25–29. **10**

Conway, Jerome K. "Information Presentation, Information Processing, and the Sign Vehicle." *Audio Visual Communication Review* 16 (1968) : 403–14. **8**

———. "Multiple-sensory Modality Communication and the problem of Sign Types." *Audio Visual Communication Review* 15 (1967) : 371–83. **3**

———. "Differential Memory for Referentially Equivalent Single and Multiple Sign-vehicle Presentations." Ph.D. dissertation, Indiana University, 1968. **3**

Cook, John Oliver, and Spitzer, Morton Edward. "Supplementary Report: Prompting Versus Confirmation in Paired-Associate Learning." *Journal of Experimental Psychology* 49, April 1960, pp. 275–76. **3**

Coone, Jim G., and White, William F. "Role of the Classroom Instructor in a Televised Introductory Psychology Course." *Psychological Reports* 23 (1968) : 43–47. **15**

Cornell, Richard A. "Understanding Computers." *Audiovisual Instruction* 14, June–July 1969, pp. 77–78. **7**

Cornett, R. Orin. *Report of a Survey of Potentialities for a College in Mobile, Alabama.* Washington: Office of Education, 1959. **14**

Cotgrove, Stephen F. *Technical Education and Social Change.* Fairlawn, N. J.: Essential Books, 1958. **1**

Coulson, John E., ed. *Programmed Learning and Computer-Based Instruction.* New York: John Wiley and Sons, 1962. **7**

Coulson, John E.; Estavan, Donald P.; Melaragno, Ralph J.; and Silberman, Harry F. "Effects of Branching in a Computer Controlled Autoinstructional Device." *Journal of Applied Psychology* 46, December 1962, pp. 389–92. **7**

Coulson, John E., and Silberman, Harry F. "Effects of Three Variables in a Teaching Machine." *Journal of Educational Psychology* 51 (1960) : 135–44. **6**

———. "Automated Teaching and Individual Differences." *Audio Visual Communication Review* 1 (1961) : 5–15. **2**

Council on Library Resources. *Automation and the Library of Congress.* Washington: Library of Congress, 1963. **6**

Cox, John A.; Melching, William H.; Jessie C.; and Smith, Robert G., Jr. *A Handbook for Programmers of Automated Instruction.* Procedural Guide, HumRRO Division No. 5 (Air Defense), Fort Bliss, Tex., September, 1963. **6**

Cram, David. *Explaining Teaching Machines and Programming.* San Francisco: Fearon Publishers, 1961. **6**

Cronbach, Lee J. "How Can Instruction Be Adapted to Individual Differences?" In *Learning and Individual Differences,* edited by R. M. Gagné. Columbus, Ohio: Charles E. Merrill Publishing Company, 1967. **13**

Crowder, Norman A. "Automatic Tutoring by Intrinsic Programming." In *Teaching Machines and Programmed Learning: A Source Book,* edited by A. A. Lumsdaine and Robert Glaser. Washington: National Education Association, 1960. **13**

———. "Simple Ways to Use the Student Response for Program Control." In *Applied Programmed Instruction,* edited by Stuart Margulies and Lewis D. Eigen. New York: John Wiley and Sons, 1962. **6**

Curl, David C. "Applications of Computer-Assisted Instruction." *Audiovisual Instruction* 13, June–July 1968, pp. 607–9. **7**

Cutler, R. L.; McKeachie, W. J.; and McNeil, E. B. "Teaching Psychology by Telephone." *American Psychologist* 13 (1958) : 551–52. **8**

Cybernetics in Education. Joint Publication Research Service, Washington, June, 1963.

Daitch, P. B. "An Experimental Course in Elementary Engineering." *Journal of Engineering Education* 59, March 1969, pp. 875–76. **13**

Dale, Edgar. "No Room for Amateurs." *Audiovisual Instruction* 6, May 1961, pp. 190–92. **12**

Das, J. P., and Pradhan, Pratibha. "Effect of Signal Satiation on Signal Detection in Auditory Vigilance." *Psychonomic Science* 13 (1968) : 211–12. **10**

David, Bro. Austin, FSC. "The Computer, Television, and Telephone As Educational Tools." *Audiovisual Instruction,* December 1968, pp. 1088–90. **4**

Davis, Gary A., and Roweton, William E. "Using Idea Checklists with College Students: Overcoming Resistance." *Journal of Psychology* 70 (1968) : 221–26. **11**

Davis, Robert H. et al. *Interaction of Individual Differences with Methods of Presenting Programed Instructional Materials by Teaching Machine and Computer: Final Report.* East Lansing: Michigan State University, Language Research Institute, 1967. **13**

DeButts, John D., *Industry Looks at Education.* New Orleans: National Association of Colleges and University Business Officers, 1967. **12**

DeKieffer, Robert E. *Audio Visual Education.* Syracuse: The Library of Education, Center for Applied Research in Education, 1963. **12**

Della-Piana, Gabriel. "An Experimental Evaluation of Programmed Learning," *Journal of Educational Research.* 55, June–July 1962, pp. 495–501. **6**

Deterline, William J. *An Introduction to Programed Instruction.* Englewood Cliffs, N. J.: Prentice-Hall, 1962. **6**

Developments in Programmed Teaching in the USSR. Joint Publication Research Service, Washington, December, 1963. **6**

Devorkin, Solomon, and Holden, Alan. "An Experimental Evaluation of Sound Film Strips vs. Classroom Lectures." *Journal Society Motion Picture TV Engineers* 68 (1959) : 383–85. **8**

Diamond, Robert M. *Programmed Instruction in Audio-Visual*

Equipment Operation and Application. Coral Gables, Fla.: University of Miami, 1965. **6**

Dick, Walter. "Retention as a Function of Paired and Individual Use of Programmed Instruction." *Journal of Programmed Instruction* 11 (1963) : 17–23. **12**

————. "The Development and Current Status of Computer Based Instruction." *American Educational Research Journal* 2 (1965) : 41–53. **7**

Diebold, John. "Obsolescence for the Printed Word?", *Think*, January–February 1969, pp. 17–19. **3**

Dolmatch, T. B. "Programmed Instruction: The Managerial Perspective." *Personnel* 39 (1962) : 45–52. **6**

Doroshkevich, A. M. *First Results of Work with a Programmed Textbook.* Washington: Joint Publication Research Service, 1964. **6**

Drahem, Edward; Trynor, Molly; and Reid, Jack. "The Computer-Mediated Instruction System at Toledo University Community and Technical College," *AEDS Monitor,* Vol. 6, Washington: Association for Educational Data Systems, October 1967, pp. 12–13. **7**

Dwyer, Francis M., Jr. "Adapting Visual Illustrations for Effective Learning." *Harvard Educational Review* 37 (1967) : 250–63. **8**

————. "The Effectiveness of Visual Illustrations Used to Complement Programed Instructions." *Journal of Psychology* 70 (1968) : 157–62. **8**

————. "Effects of Varying Amount of Realistic Detail in Visual Illustrations Designed to Complement Programmed Instruction." *Perceptual and Motor Skills* 27 (1968) : 351–354. **13**

Eckert, Sidney W. The Effect of the Use of Overhead Transparencies on Achievement and Retention in General Business. *Dissertation Abstracts A,* vol. 28, pp. 4946–47. Ann Arbor, Mich.: University Microfilms, 1968. **8**

Educational Technology 8, May 1968. **1**

"The Educational Technology Act of 1968." *Educational Technology,* January 1969, pp. 34–39. **3**

Educational Television Bibliography. Pleasantville, N. Y.: General Precision, GPL Division, August 1968. **8**

" 'Educational TV'—A Progress Report." *U. S. News and World Report* 66, 9 June 1969, p. 46. **8**

Egbert, Robert L., and Cogswell, John F. *System Analysis and Design in Schools.* Santa Monica, Calif.: System Development Corporation, March, 1963. **2**

Eibler, H. J. "Characteristics for Innovation." *Clearing House,* 43, May 1969, pp. 523–26. **11**

Eigen, Lewis D., and Margulies, Stuart. "Response Characteristics as a Function of Information Level." *Journal of Programmed Instruction* 2 (1963) : 45–54. **10**

Elley, Warwick B. "The Role of Errors in Learning with Feedback." *British Journal of Educational Psychology* 36 (1966) : 296–300. **10**

Ely, Donald P., ed. "The Changing Role of the Audiovisual Process in Education: A Definition and a Glossary of Related Terms," *Audio Visual Communication Review* 11, January–February 1963. **4**

English, R. A., and Kinger, J. R. "The Effect of Immediate and Delayed Feedback on Retention of Subject Matter." *Psychology in the Schools* 3 (1966) : 143–47. **10**

Entelek Computer-Assisted Instruction Guide. Newburyport, Mass.: Entelek, 1968. **7**

Entelek Computer-Based Math Lab. Newburyport, Mass.: Entelek, 1969. **7**

Erickson, C. G. "The Administrator, Educational Problems, and Instructional Television." In *A Guide to Instructional Television,* edited by Robert M. Diamond. New York: McGraw-Hill Book Company, 1964. **8**

Erickson, Carlton W. H. *Administering Instructional Media Programs.* New York: MacMillan Company, 1968. **5**

————. "The Making of New School Media Specialists—From the Audiovisual Point of View." *Audiovisual Instruction,* January 1969, pp. 14–19. **12**

Esper, Erwin A., and Lovass, O. Ivar. "The Effect of Verbal Symbolization on the Serial Position Curve in Motor Perceptual Maze Learning." *Journal of General Psychology* 66, January 1962, pp. 47–55. **3**

ETV: A Ford Foundation Pictorial Report. New York: Ford Foundation, 1961. **8**

Eurich, Alvin C., ed. *Campus, 1980.* New York: Dell Publishing Company, 1968. **14**

Eurich, Alvin C. "The Commitment to Experiment and Innovation in College Teaching." *The Educational Record* 45 (1964) : 49. **11**

Eurich, Alvin C. "A 21st-Century Look at Higher Education." *Liberal Education* 49, March 1963, pp. 22–33. **1**

Evans, James L. "Programing in Mathematics and Logic." In *Teaching Machines and Programmed Learning,* Vol. 2, edited by

Robert Glaser, pp. 371–440. Washington: National Education Association, Department of Audiovisual Instruction, 1966. **6**

Evans, James L; Glaser, Robert; and Homme, Lloyd E. "An Investigation of 'Teaching Machine' Variables Using Learning Programs in Symbolic Logic." *Journal of Educational Research* 55, June–July 1962, pp. 433–52. **6**

Evans, Richard I., and Leppmann, Peter K. *Resistance to Innovation in Higher Education: A Social Psychological Exploration Focused on Television and the Establishment.* San Francisco: Jossey-Bass, 1968. **11**

Evans, Richard I.; Smith, R. G.; and Colville, W. K. *The University Faculty and Educational Television: Hostility, Resistance, and Change.* Houston: University of Houston, 1962. **8**

Evans, Richard I.; Wieland, B. A.; and Moore, C. W. "The Effect of Experience In Telecourses on Attitudes Toward Instruction by Television and Impact of a Controversial Television Program." *Journal of Applied Psychology* 45 (1961) : 11–15. **8**

Evans, Robert C. *Higher Education and Unemployment—Some Paradoxes.* Calif.: San Jose State College, 1966. **12**

Everly, Jack C. "Continuing Education Instruction Via the Mass Media." Paper presented at the National Seminar on Adult Education Research. Urbana: University of Illinois, 1968. **13**

Everote, Warren. "Forty Years After the Audiovisual Revolution." *Audiovisual Instruction* 14, April 1969, pp. 88–93. **1**

Eyertone, Merle L. "A Comparison of the Effectiveness of Bulletin, Film, and Lecture with and without Discussing in Presenting Research Information." Ph.D. dissertation, University of Wisconsin, 1966. **13**

A Fact Sheet Concerning Closed Circuit Instructional Television for English Language Teaching. Seoul, South Korea: Sogang Jesuit College, 1967. **7**

Fall, Charles R. *Individualizing University Instruction: Exploring Computer Potential to Aid College Teachers by Directing the Learning Process.* Inter-University Project One, Publications Series. Buffalo: State University of New York, College at Buffalo, 1968. **7**

Farrell, Edmund J. *English, Education and the Electronic Revolution.* Champaign, Ill.: National Council of Teachers of English, 1967. **1**

Faust, Gerald W. "The Effects of Prompting in Programmed Instruction as a Function of Motivation and Instructions." Ph.D. dissertation, University of Illinois, 1968. **10**

Feldhusen, John F. "The Effects of Small and Large Group Instruction on Learning of Subject Matter, Attitudes, and Interests." *Journal of Psychology* 55, April 1963, pp. 357–62. **15**

Feldhusen, John F., and Birt, Andrew. "A Study of Nine Methods of Presentation of Programmed Learning Material." *Journal of Educational Research* 55, June–July 1962, pp. 461–66. **6**

Feldman, Margaret E. "Learning by Programmed and Text Format at Three Levels of Difficulty." *Journal of Educational Psychology* 56 (1965) : 133–39. **6**

Feroter, C. B. "A Semi-Automatic Teaching Machine." *Journal of Experimental Analysis of Behavior* 3 (1960) : 245–46. **6**

Finn, James D. "Automation and Education III Technology and the Instructional Process." *Audio Visual Communication Review* 8 (1960) : 5–26. **1**

———. "A New Theory for Instructional Technology." *Audio Visual Communication Review* 8 (1960) : 84–94. **1**

———. "A Possible Model for Considering the Use of Media in Higher Education." *Audio Visual Communication Review* 15 (1967) : 153–57. **9**

Finn, James D.; and Bolvin, Boyd M.; and Perrin, Donald G. *A Selective Bibliography on New Media and Instructional Technology.* Staff Paper Number One, Instructional Technology and Media Project, School of Education, Los Angeles: University of Southern California, 1964. **2**

Finn, James D., and Perrin, Donald G. *Teaching Machines and Programmed Learning, 1962: A Survey of the Industry.* Occasional Paper No. 3, National Education Association Technological Development Project. Washington, D.C.: National Education Association, 1961. **6**

Fischer, John H. "The Teacher's Role Growing." *New York Times,* 12 January 1968, p. 74. **15**

Fleischer, Eugene B. "Uniterm Your Audiovisual Library." *Audiovisual Instruction,* February 1969, pp. 76–78. **5**

Fleming, Malcolm. "Classification and Analysis of Instructional Illustrations." *Audio Visual Communication Review* 15, Fall 1967, pp. 246–58. **2**

Fleming, Malcolm L. et al. *Message Design: The Temporal Dimension of Message Structure: Final Report.* Bloomington, Ind.: Indiana University, 1968. **3**

Flynn, John T. "The Influence of Programmed Instruction Upon Learning in Educational Psychology." *Journal of Educational Research* 59 (1966) : 387–91. **13**

Follettie, J. F. *Effects of Training Response Mode, Test Form, and*

Measure on Acquisition of Semi-Ordered Factual Materials. Research Memorandum, HumRRO Division No. 4 (Infantry), Fort Benning, Ga., 1961. **3**

Fox, Raymond B. "Innovations in Education," *Illinois Education Association Discussion Topic* 31, March 1969. **11**

Freedman, Morris. "Toward a Science of Educational Communications." *Audiovisual Instruction* 14, April 1969, p. 112. **2**

Frick, F. C., and Sumby, W. H. "Control Tower Language." In *Some Theories of Organization,* edited by Albert H. Rubenstein and Chadwick J. Haverstroh. Homewood, Ill.: Dorsey Press, 1960. **3**

Fry, Edward B. *Teaching Machines and Programmed Instruction.* New York: McGraw Hill Book Company, 1963. **6**

Fry, Edward B.; Bryan, Glenn L.; and Rigney, Joseph W. "Teaching Machines: An Annotated Bibliography," *Audio Visual Communication Review,* vol. 8, no. 2, *Supplement* (1960) : 1–80. **2**

Frymire, Lawrence T. "Illinois Telecommunications Research Project." *Audiovisual Instruction,* December 1968, pp. 1068–70. **13**

Gage, N. L., ed. *Handbook of Research on Teaching.* Chicago: Rand McNally and Company, 1963. **2**

Gagné, Robert M., ed. *Learning and Individual Differences.* Columbus, Ohio: Charles E. Merrill Publishing Company, 1967. **3**

Gagné, Robert M. "The Learning Requirements for Enquiry." *Journal of Research in Scientific Teaching* 1 (1963) : 144–53. **3**

———. "Problem Solving." In *Categories of Human Learning,* edited by A. W. Melton. New York: Academic Press, 1964. **3**

Gagné, Robert M., and Brown, L. T. "Some Factors in the Programing of Conceptual Learning." *Journal of Experimental Psychology* 62 (1961) : 313–21. **6**

Gagné, Robert M., and Smith, Ernest C., Jr. "A Study of the Effects of Verbalization on Problem Solving." *Journal of Experimental Psychology* 63, January 1962, pp. 12–18. **3**

Galanter, Eugene, ed. *Automatic Teaching: The State of the Art.* New York: John Wiley and Sons, 1959. **6**

Gay, Robert T. *An Evaluation of the Effect of an Immediate Feedback Device Used with Typical College Classroom Tests: Final Report.* San Diego, Calif.: San Diego State College, 1967. **10**

Genesys (Graduate Engineering Education System) 20. Gainesville: University of Florida, College of Engineering, January, 1966. **8**

Gentile, J. Ronald. "The First Generation of Computer-Assisted Instructional Systems: An Evaluative Review." *Audio Visual Communication Review* 15, Spring, 1967, pp. 23–53. **7**

Gerlach, Vernon S. "The Professional Education of the Media Specialist." *Audio Visual Communication Review* 14, Summer 1966, pp. 185–201. **12**

Giacalone, Carolyn, and Davis, Dolores. *Research in International Education—Research in Progress and Research Recently Completed: 1966–67 Survey.* New York: National Association for Foreign Student Affairs, Institute of International Education, 1967. **14**

Gilbert, T. F. "On the Relevance of Laboratory Investigation of Learning to Self-Instructional Programming." In *Teaching Machines and Programmed Learning: A Source Book,* edited by A. A. Lumsdaine and Robert Glaser. Washington: National Education Association, 1960. **3**

Gilman, David A. *A Comparison of the Effectiveness of Feedback Modes for Teaching Science Concepts by Means of a Computer Assisted Adjunct Auto-Instruction Program.* University Park: Pennsylvania State University, 1968. **10**

Gilman, David A., and Moreau, Nancy Ann. "Effects of Reducing Verbal Content in Computer-Assisted Instruction." *Audio Visual Communication Review* 17, Fall 1969, pp. 291–98. **7**

Goldstein, Leo S., and Gotkin, Lassar G. "A Review of Research: Teaching Machines vs. Programed Textbooks as Presentation Modes." *Journal of Programed Instruction* 1 (1962) : 29–36. **6**

Goodman, Jesse. "Programmed Instruction, Remedial Treatment, and Resistance to Learning: An Experimental and Exploratory Study of Facilitating and Hindering Factors in Remedial Programmed Instruction." Ph.D. dissertation, New York University, 1967. **6**

Gordon, Edmund W. The Higher Education of the Disadvantaged. New Dimensions in Higher Education, no. 28. Durham, N. C.: Duke University, 1967. **13**

Gordon, Roger L. "The Urban Concentric Media Plan: A Model for Today." *Audiovisual Instruction,* 14, December 1969, pp. 50–51. **14**

Gornick, Richard. "A Study of the Relationship Between Conceptual Framework and the Transference of Learning in the Social Studies." *Dissertation Abstracts A,* vol. 29, p. 511. Ann Arbor, Mich.: University Microfilms, 1968. **2**

Gorrow, Frank F. "Teaching Machine Theory Applied to Learning Statistics." *California Journal of Educational Research* 12 (1961) : 67–71. **6**

Goss, Albert E. "Acquisition and Use of Conceptual Schemes." In

Verbal Learning and Verbal Behavior, edited by C. N. Cofer. New York: McGraw-Hill Book Company, 1961. **2**

Gottschalk, Gunther H. *Closed Circuit Television in Second Semester College German.* New York: National Federation of Modern Language Teachers Association, 1965. **8**

Graham, G. L. "Teacher's Adventures in Programland." *English Journal* 58, February 1969, pp. 261–66. **6**

Green, Alan C., ed. *Educational Facilities with New Media.* Washington: Department of Audiovisual Instruction, National Education Association, 1966. **14**

Green, Edward J. *The Learning Process and Programmed Instruction.* New York: Holt, Rinehart and Winston, 1962. **6**

Griessman, B. Eugene. "An Approach to Evaluating Comprehensive Social Projects," *Educational Technology* 9, February 1969, pp. 16–19. **3**

Grindeland, William D. "The Development of a Multi-Media Kit Program." *Audiovisual Instruction,* October, 1968, pp. 865–67. **13**

Gropper, George L. "Does 'Programed' Television Need Active Responding?" *Audio Visual Communication Review* 15 (1967) : 5–22. **10**

———. "Learning from Visuals: Some Behavioral Considerations." *Audio Visual Communication Review* 14, Spring 1966, pp. 37–69. **8**

Gropper, George L., and Lumsdaine, A. A. *An Experimental Comparison of A Conventional TV Lesson with a Programmed TV Lesson Requiring Active Student Response: Studies in Televised Instruction, Report No. 2, USOE Project No. 336.* Pittsburgh: Metropolitan Pittsburgh Education Television Station WQED-WQEX and American Institutes for Research, 1961. **8**

Gryde, Stanley K. "The Feasibility of "Programed" Television Instruction." *Audio Visual Communication Review* 14, Spring 1966, pp. 71–89. **8**

Guerin, David V. "Implications for the Communications Process for School Plant Design." *Audiovisual Instruction* 12 (1967): 815–17. **14**

———. "Media's Influence on Design." *Audiovisual Instruction,* February 1965, pp. 95–97. **14**

Guilford, J. P. *The Nature of Human Intelligence.* New York: McGraw-Hill Book Company, 1967. **3**

Haefele, Donald L. "Self-Instruction and Teacher Education." *Audiovisual Instruction,* vol. 14, no. 1, January 1969, pp. 63–64. **13**

Haga, Eenoch. *Automated Educational Systems,* Elmhurst, Ill.: Business Press, 1967. **6**

Haines, Donald B., and McKeachie, W. J. "Cooperative vs. Competitive Discussion Methods in Teaching Introductory Psychology." *Journal of Educational Psychology* 58 (1967) : 386–90. **15**

Hall, Edward T. *The Hidden Dimension.* Garden City, N. Y.: Doubleday And Company, 1966. **11**

Hamblen, John W. "Education and the Computer—Pluses and Minuses in the Educational Equation." *AED Monitor* 6, October 1967, pp. 14–16. **7**

———. *Computers in Higher Education—Expenditures, Sources of Funds, and Utilization for Research and Instruction 1964–65, with Projections for 1968–69: A Report on a Survey.* Atlanta: Southern Regional Education Board, 1967. **7**

Hamlin, Will, and Porter, Lawrence. *Dimensions of Changes in Higher Education, Workshop Conferences to foster Innovation in Higher Education* (1st, Magnolia Manor, Massachusetts, May 19–23, 1966). Union for Research and Experimentation in Higher Education, 1967. **11**

Hammond, Robert. "Context Evaluation of Instruction in Local School Districts." *Educational Technology* 9, January 1969, pp. 13–18. **14**

Haney, John B.; Lange, Phil C.; and Barson, John. "The Heuristic Dimension of Instructional Development." *Audio Visual Communication Review* 16, Winter 1966, pp. 358–71. **1**

Harcleroad, Fred F. "Theoretical Formulations in Audiovisual Communications." *Review of Educational Research* 32, April 1962, pp. 119–26. **3**

Harcleroad, Fred F. et al. *Learning Resources for Colleges and Universities.* Hayward, Calif.: California State College, 1964. **5**

Harding, Robert G. "New Dimensions to School-Produced Media." *Audiovisual Instruction* 14, April 1969, p. 65. **5**

Hartman, F. R. "Recognition Learning Under Multiple Channel Presentation." *Audio Visual Communication Review* 9 (1961): 24–43. **3**

Hatfield, Robert C. "Designing and Instructional Strategy." *Educational Technology* 9, February 1969, pp. 37–38. **6**

Hauf, Harold D. et al. *New Spaces for Learning.* Troy, N. Y.: School of Architecture, Rensselaer Polytechnic Institute, 1961. **14**

Hickey, Albert E. *Computer Assisted Instruction: A Survey of the Literature.* 3d ed. Newburyport, Mass.: Entelek, Incorporated, 1968. **12**

Higher Education Facilities Inventory Manual. Washington State
Higher Education Facilities Commission, 1967. **14**

Hill, Edwin K. "The Development and Testing of an Experimental
Polysensory Self-Instructional System Designed to Help Students
Acquire Basic Electrical Occupational Competencies." Ph.D. dis-
sertation, Washington State University, 1968. **2**

Hill, Walker H. *An Analysis of the Radio-Television Training Programs in Institutions of Higher Education.* East Lansing: Michigan
State University, 1960. **8**

Hively, W. "Programming Stimuli in Matching to Sample." *Journal
of Experimental and Analytical Behavior* 5 (1962) : 279–98. **6**

———. "Specifying 'Terminal Behavior' in Mathematics." Mimeographed. Cambridge, Mass.: Harvard University, 1962. **10**

Hochberg, Julian E. *Perception.* Englewood Cliffs, N. J.: Prentice-
Hall, 1964. **3**

Hodgkinson, Harold et al. *Bard Corrects Freshmen Themes on Tape.*
Washington: American Association for Higher Education,
1968. **13**

Hodgson, James B., Jr. *ICAF-Temper 66, Student Acceptance of a
Computer Simulation of International Relations as an Adjunct to
the Curriculum of the Industrial College of the Armed Forces.*
Operations Research Systems Engineering. Washington: American
Council on Education, 1966. **9**

Holland, James G. "A Quantitative Measure for Programmed Instruction." *American Educational Research Journal* 4 (1967) : 87–
102. **6**

Holland, James G., and Porter, Douglas. "The Influence of Repeti-
tion of Incorrectly Answered Items in a Teaching-Machine Program." *Journal of Experimental and Analytical Behavior* 4 (1961) :
305–07. **3**

Holland, James G., and Skinner. B. F. *The Analysis of Behavior: A
Program for Self Instruction.* New York: McGraw Hill Book Company, 1961. **6**

Holloway, P. J. "The Effect of Lecture Time on Learning." *British
Journal of Educational Psychology* 36 (1966) : 255–58. **10**

Holtzman, Wayne H. *The University of Texas Laboratory for Computer Assisted Instruction.* Austin, Tex.: University of Texas,
1967. **7**

Homme, L. E., and Glaser, R. "Problems in Programming Verbal
Learning Sequences." In *Teaching Machines and Programmed
Learning: A Source Book,* edited by A. A. Lumsdaine and

R. Glaser. Washington: National Education Association, 1960. **13**

Hooper, Richard. "A Diagnosis of Failure." *Audio Visual Communication Review* 17, Fall 1969, pp. 245–64. **1**

Hough, John B. "An Analysis of the Efficiency and Effectiveness of Selected Aspects of Machine Instruction." *Journal of Educational Research* 55, June–July 1962, pp. 467–71. **6**

Howe, Harold, II. U. S. Commissioner of Education, U. S. Department of Health, Education, and Welfare. *The People Who Serve Education: A Report on the State of the Education Professions.* Washington: U. S. Government Printing Office, 1968. **15**

Hsia, Hower J. "Output, Error, Equivocation, and Recalled Information in Auditory, Visual, and Audiovisual Information Processing and Constraint and Noise." *Journal of Communication* 18 (1968) : 325–53. **10**

Hughes, J. L., and McNamara, W. J. "A Comparative Study of Programed and Conventional Instruction in Industry." *Journal of Applied Psychology* 45, August 1961, pp. 225–31. **6**

Hughes, J. P. *The Science of Language.* New York: Random House, 1962. **3**

Hulett, J. Edward, Jr., "A Symbolic Interactionist Model of Human Communication." *Audio Visual Communication Review* 14, Spring 1966, pp. 5–33; 14, Summer 1966, pp. 203–220. **9**

"The Impact of Technology on the Library Building." A position paper prepared for Educational Facilities Laboratories, New York, 1967. **14**

Ingham, George E. "Preservice Media Training." *Audiovisual Instruction,* January 1969, pp. 55–57. **5**

Ingraham, Leonard W. "Instructional Technology—New Strategies and Roles for the Social Studies Teacher." *Audiovisual Instruction* 14, April 1969, pp. 24–25. **15**

Innovation in Education: New Directions for the American School, Committee for Economic Development, New York, 1968. **11**

Jackson, Philip W. *The Teacher and the Machine.* Pittsburgh, Pa.: University of Pittsburgh Press, 1968. **15**

Jamrich, John X. *To Build or Not to Build.* New York: Educational Facilities Laboratory, 1963. **14**

Jernigan, Elizabeth Thorne. "Computer-Assisted Instruction for Teaching Library Processes," *AEDS Monitor* 6, October 1967, pp. 3–4. **7**

Johnson, F. Craig, "Feedback: Principles and Analogies." *Journal of Communication* 12, September 1962, pp. 150–59. **10**

Johnson, H. B. *A Comparative Study of an Introductory Geography Course on ETV and in Classroom.* St. Paul, Minn.: Macalester College, 1960. **8**

Johnson, Lamar. "Encouraging Innovation in Teaching." *Junior College Journal* 39, March 1969, pp. 18–22. **11**

Johnson, Rita B. "The Effects of Prompting Practice and Feedback in Programmed Videotape." *American Educational Research Journal* 5 (1968) : 73–79. **10**

Jordan, James R. *The National Center for School and College Television—A Demonstration of a National Program Agency for Instructional Television: Final Report.* Bloomington: Indiana University Foundation, 1968. **8**

Kagan, Jerome; Rosman, Bernice L.; Day, Deborah; Albert, Joseph; and Phillips, William. "Information Processing in the Child: Significance of Analytic and Reflective Attitudes." *Psychological Monographs: General and Applied,* vol. 78, no. 1, edited by Gregory A. Kimble. Washington: American Psychological Association, 1964. **3**

Kanfer, Frederick H., and Marston, Albert R. "Human Reinforcement: Vicarious and Direct." *Journal of Experimental Psychology* 65, March 1963, pp. 292–96. **3**

Kanner, J. W., and Wesley, P. M. "Television in Basic Training: The Improvement of Training by Television." *Audio Visual Communication Review* 11 (1963) : 191–99. **8**

Kantasewi, Niphon, and McClay, David R. *Experiments in the Use of Programed Materials in Teaching an Elementary College Course in the Biological Sciences.* Teacher Education Research Series, vol. 5, no. 1. University Park: Pennsylvania State University, 1964. **6**

Kaska, John. "Technical Applications of a Concept of Multiple Reality." *The International Journal of Psychoanalysis* 45 (1964) : 575–78. **3**

Katz, E. "The Social Itinerary of Technical Change: Two Studies on the Diffusion of Innovation." *Human Organization* 20 (1961) : 70–82. **11**

Kaufman, R. A.; Corrigan, R. E.; Corrigan, B. O.; and Goodwin, D. L. *Steps and Tools of System Analysis as Applied to Education; Steps and Tools of the System Synthesis Process in Education; Mission Analysis in Education; Functional Analysis in Education; Task Analysis in Education; Methods-means Analysis in Education; An Interim Generic Problem Solving Model; An Exercise in the Analysis of Planned Change in Education* (Eight pamphlets prepared for Operation PEP) San Mateo, Calif.: San Mateo County Department of Education, 1967. **2**

Keller, Fred S. "Good-bye Teacher." *Journal of Applied Behavior Analysis* 1 (1968) : 79–89. **15**

————. "Engineering Personalized Instruction in the Classroom." *Revista Interamericana de Psicologia* 1 (1967) : 189–97. **15**

Kerr, Eugene G., and Rahmlow, Harold F. "Computer-Assisted Math Instruction in Small Schools." *Audiovisual Instruction,* February 1969, pp. 24–26. **7**

Ketcham, Carl H., and Heath, Robert W. "Teaching Effectiveness of Sound with Pictures that Do Not Embody the Material Being Taught." *Audio Visual Communication Review* 10 (1962) : 89–93. **8**

Kight, Howard R., and Sassenrath, Julius M. "Relation of Achievement Motivation and Test Anxiety to Performance in Programed Instruction." *Journal of Educational Psychology* 57, (1966) : pp. 14–17. **6**

Killory, John F. "A Teaching Machine for Counselor Education." Ph.D. dissertation, University of Wisconsin, 1968. **13**

King, Gilbert W., ed. *Automation and the Library of Congress.* Washington: Library of Congress, 1963. **2**

Kirk, Samuel A. "A Model of a Communication Process." *Report of the Proceedings of the International Congress on Education of the Deaf and of the 41st Meeting of the Convention of American Instructors of the Deaf.* In Senate Document no. 106, 88th Congress, Second Session, Washington: Government Printing Office, 1964, pp. 450–57. **9**

Klaus, D. J. "The Art of Auto-Instructional Programming." *Audio Visual Communications Review* 9 (1961) : 130–42. **6**

Knight, Melvin E., and Smith, Dennis L. "Teaching the Effective Use of Media." *Audiovisual Instruction,* January, 1969, pp. 29–30. **5**

Knowlton, James Q. *A Socio- and Psycho-Linguistic Theory of Pictorial Communication.* Bloomington: Indiana University, Division of Education Media and Audio-Visual Center, 1964. **3**

————. "A Conceptual Scheme for the Audiovisual Field." *Bulletin of the School of Education* 40, Indiana University (1964) : 1–42. **3**

Koch, Cyril M. "The Systems Model in Practice." *Audiovisual Instruction* 14, June–July 1969, p. 73. **2**

Kopstein, F. F. *The Amplified Teacher: The Guidance of Human Learning Through Controlling Functional Automata.* Research

Memorandum, RM-65-15, Princeton, N. J.: Educational Testing Service, 1965. **15**

Kopstein, F. F., and Carbe, R. T. *Preliminary Cost Comparison of Technical Training by Conventional and Programmed Learning Methods: Technical Documentary Report MRL-TDR-62-79.* Wright-Patterson Air Force Base, Ohio: Behavioral Science Laboratory, Aeromedical Division, July, 1962. **6**

Kopstein, F. F., and Seidel, Robert J. "Computer-Administered Instruction Versus Traditionally Administered Instruction: Economics." *Audio Visual Communication Review* 16, Summer 1968, pp. 147–75. **7**

Krech, David. "The Chemistry of Learning." *Saturday Review* 51, 20 January 1968, pp. 48–50. **3**

Kress, Gerard C., Jr. *A Study of Social Facilitation During Programed Instruction.* Proceedings of the 75th Annual Convention of the American Psychological Association, 1967, pp. 313–314. **15**

Kress, Gerard C., Jr., and Gropper, G. L. "A Comparison of Two Strategies for Individualizing Fixed-Paced Programmed Instruction." *American Educational Research Journal* 3 (1966) : 273–80. **6**

Krumboltz, John D. "Meaningful Learning and Retention: Practice and Reinforcement Variables." *Review of Educational Research* 31, December 1961, pp. 535–46. **3**

Krumboltz, John D., and Weisman, Ronald G. "The Effect of Overt vs. Covert Responding to Programmed Instruction on Immediate and Delayed Retention." *Journal of Educational Psychology* 53 (1962) : 89–92. **10**

Kulik, V. T. *Group Studies with the Use of Programmed Texts.* Washington: Joint Publication Research Service, 1964. **6**

Kumata, Hideya. *Attitude Change and Learning as a Function of Prestige of Instructor and Mode of Presentation: Two Experimental Studies in Instructional Television.* East Lansing: Michigan State University, College of Communications, 1958. **15**

———. "New Media-Research Findings in the U. S. A." In *Communication Media and the Schools.* World Yearbook of Education. Edited by George Z. F. Bereday and D. Lauwerys. Tarrytown-on-Hudson, N. Y.: World Publishing Company, 1960. **3**

Kurland, Norman. "What Is Innovation?" *Educational Technology,* February 1969, pp. 35–36. **11**

Lange, Phil C. "Media and the Learning Process." *Audiovisual Instruction* 13, June–July 1968, pp. 554–57. **4**

Larson, L. C. "Developing a Graduate Program to Train Instructional Design and Media Specialists." *Audiovisual Instruction,* January 1969, pp. 20–24. **12**

Lebedev, P. D. *Computers for Education.* Washington: Joint Publication Research Service, 1963. **7**

Lekan, Helen, ed. *Index to Computer Assisted Instruction.* Milwaukee: University of Wisconsin, Instruction Media Laboratory, February 1969. **7**

Lepore, Albert R., and Wilson, Jack D. *Instructional Television Research Project Number Two: An Experimental Study of College Instruction Using Broadcast Television.* San Francisco: San Francisco State College, Station KQED, 1958. **8**

Lescarbeau, Roland F. et al. *A Suggested Curriculum Guide for Electro-Mechanical Technology Oriented Specifically to the Computer and Business Machine Fields: Interim Report.* Hartford, Conn.: Hartford University, War Technical Institute, 1968. **7**

Lesser, Gerald S., and Schueler, Herbert. "New Media Research in Teacher Education." *Audio Visual Communication Review* 14, Fall 1966, pp. 318–61. **3**

Levonian, Edward, "Development of an Audience-Tailored Film." *Audio Visual Communication Review* 8 (1960) : 62–68. **8**

Liberman, Herbert, and Swope, Watson. "Analyzing Student Behavioral Patterns with CCTV." *Audiovisual Instruction,* November 1969, pp. 50–51. **7**

Lippincott, W. T., and Brasted, R. C. *Modern Teaching Aids for College Chemistry—Portable Video Recording Systems: New Uses for Films, Computer Assisted Instruction.* Washington: Advisory Council on College Chemistry, 1966. **5**

Lombard, Bruce A. "The Relationship Between Self Concept and Oral Contribution." Ph.D. dissertation, University of South Dakota, 1968. **15**

Lumsdaine, A. A. "Design of Teaching Aids and Devices." In *Human Factors Methods for System Design,* edited by John D. Folley, Jr. Pittsburgh: American Institute for Research, 1960. **4**

———. "Instruments and Media of Instruction." In *Handbook of Research on Teaching,* edited by N. L. Gage. Chicago: Rand McNally and Company, 1963. **4**

Lumsdaine, A. A., and Glaser, Robert, eds. *Teaching Machines and Programmed Learning: A Source Book.* Washington: Department of Audiovisual Instruction, National Education Association, 1960. **6**

McBride, Wilma, ed. *The James Madison Wood Quadrangle: Stephens College.* Columbia, Mo.: Stephens College, 1964. **14**

McBride, Otis. "Learning Through Media in the Library." *Audiovisual Instruction,* January 1969, p. 69. **5**

McCartan, Edward F. "EDUCOM and the Applications of Technology." *Audiovisual Instruction,* December 1968, pp. 1071–73. **5**

Macomber, F. G., *Experimental Study in Instructional Procedures.* Oxford, Ohio: Miami University, 1956. **5**

————. *Experimental Study in Instructional Procedures: Second Report.* Oxford, Ohio: Miami University, 1957. **5**

McDonald, Frederick J., and Allen, Dwight W. "An Investigation of Presentation, Response, and Correction Factors in Programmed Instruction." *Journal of Educational Research* 55, June–July 1962, pp. 502–07. **6**

McGrew, J. M.; Marcia, J. E.; and Wright, C. K. "Branching Program, Text, and Lecture: A Comparative Investigation of Instructional Media." *Journal of Applied Psychology* 50 (1966) : 505–08. **4**

McIntire, Roger W. "Reinforcement and Verbal Learning: A Test of the Premack Hypothesis." *Psychological Reports* 12, February 1963, pp. 99–102. **3**

McIntyre, Charles J., and Haney, John B. *A Study of the Implications and Feasibility of the Full Application of Technological Aids to the Solution of Staff, Space, and Curriculum Problems Associated with a Rapidly Growing Urban University: Final Report.* Chicago: University of Illinois, 1967. **14**

McKay, William. "Computer-Directed Instructional Games." *Audiovisual Instruction* 14, April 1969, pp. 37–40. **7**

McKeachie, W. J. "Interaction of Achievement Cues and Facilitating Anxiety in the Achievement of Women." *Journal of Applied Psychology* 53 (1969) : 147–48. **10**

————. "Procedures and Techniques of Teaching: A Survey of Experimental Studies." In *The American College: A Psychological and Social Interpretation of the Higher Learning,* edited by Nevitt Sanford. New York: John Wiley and Sons, 1962. **13**

————. "Psychology at Age 75: The Psychology Teacher Comes into his Own." *American Psychologist* 23 (1968) : 551–57. **15**

————. "Understanding the Learning Process." *Journal of Engineering Education* 51, February 1961, pp. 405–08. **1**

McKeefery, William J. "The Impact of Effective Utilization of Faculty and Facilities on the Changing Role of the Professor." *Current Issues in Higher Education* (1966) : 226–31. **15**

McKenney, James L., and Dill, William R. "Influences on Learning in Simulation Games." *American Behavioral Scientist* 10 (1966) : 28–32. **9**

McLaragno, Ralph J. "Effect of Negative Reinforcement in an Automated Teaching Setting." *Psychological Reports* 7, October 1960, pp. 381–84. **13**

McLuhan, H. Marshall. *Understanding Media: The Extensions of Man.* New York: McGraw-Hill Book Company, 1964. **1**

——. "Electronics and the Changing Role of Print." *Audio Visual Communication Review* 8 (1960) : 74–83. **1**

McNeil, John. "An Experimental Effort to Improve Instruction Through Visual Feedback." *Journal of Educational Research* 55 (1962) : 283–85. **10**

Mager, Robert F. *Preparing Objectives for Programmed Instruction.* San Francisco: Fearon Publishers, 1961. **6**

——. *Preparing Instructional Objectives.* Palo Alto, Calif.: Fearon Publishers, 1962. **1**

——. "Engineering of Behavior." *Journal of Engineering Education* 59, March 1969, pp. 841–43. **12**

Mahaffy, Carolyn T. "Expanding Limited Lives with Media." *Audiovisual Instruction,* November 1969, pp. 34–36. **15**

Main, Jeremy. "Computer Time-Sharing—Everyman at the Console." *Fortune,* August 1967, pp. 88–91; 187–190. **7**

Maltz, Maxwell. *Psycho-Cybernetics.* Englewood Cliffs, N. J.: Prentice-Hall, 1960. **1**

Maltzman, Irving. "On the Training of Originality." *Psychological Reviews* 67, July 1960, pp. 229–42. **11**

Margoles, Richard Allan, "Guideline for Implementing Media Support Services at the College Level." *Audiovisual Instruction,* November 1969, pp. 69–71. **5**

Marlow, Forster L. "The Effect of Classroom Role Interactions on Visual and Verbal Measures of Educational Attitudes, Questioning Power, and Studio Art Work of Elementary Education Majors." Ph.D. dissertation, Pennsylvania State University, 1966. **15**

Martin, John R. et al. *Studies in Educational Closed-Circuit Television.* Cleveland: Case Institute of Technology, 1958. **8**

Martin, Warren Bryan. "Inclusive Innovation." *The Research Reporter* 2 (1967) : 15 pp. **11**

Martinson, John. "Information Technology and the Community College Curricula." *Audiovisual Instruction* 14, March 1969, pp. 65–67. **5**

Mattox, Robert F. *Computer Modeling in Campus Design: Case*

Study at Duke University: Final Paper. Washington: American Institute of Architects, 1967. **9**

———. *Planning the Campus by Computer.* Montclair, N. J.: *Architectural and Engineering News,* December 1968. **14**

Mauch, James. "A Systems Analysis Approach to Education." *Phi Delta Kappan* 43, January 1962, pp. 158–62. **2**

Mayers, Alan E. "The Effects of Student Location and Teacher Role on Learning from Instructional Television." Ph.D. dissertation, Stanford University, 1966. **14**

Mayzner, M. S.; Tresselt, M. E.; and Helfor, M. S. "A Provisional Model of Visual Information Processing with Sequential Inputs." *Psychronomic Monograph Supplements* 2 (1967) : 91–108. **9**

Mechner, F. *Programming for Automated Instruction.* New York: Basic Systems, 1961. **6**

Meierhenry, Wesley C. "Innovation, Education, and Media." *Audio Visual Communication Review* 14, Winter 1966, pp. 451–65. **11**

———. "Editor's Foreword: Learning Theory and AV Utilization." *Audio Visual Communication Review* 9, September–October 1961, pp. 3–6. **3**

———. "Media Competencies for Teachers." *Audiovisual Instruction,* vol. 14, no. 4, Winter 1966, pp. 451–65; vol. 9, no. 5, September–October 1961, Supplement 4. **15**

Melaragno, Ralph J. "Effect of Negative Reinforcement in an Automated Teaching Setting." *Psychological Reports* 7 (1960) : 381–84. **6**

Menzel, Herbert et al. "The Effectiveness of the Televised Clinical Seminars of the New York Academy of Medicine, 1966." *Bulletin of the New York Academy of Medicine.* Second Series, vol. 42, no. 8, December 1968. **8**

Meyer, Susan R. "A Test of the Principle of 'Activity,' 'Immediate Reinforcement,' and 'Guidance' As Instrumented by Skinner's Teaching Machine." Ph.D. dissertation, University of Buffalo, 1960. **3**

Michael, Donald N., *Cybernation: The Silent Conquest.* Santa Barbara, Calif.: Center for the Study of Democratic Institutions, 1962. **1**

Mild, J. Donald, and Dought, Donald D. *A Communications System for Higher Education: Final Report.* Dominquez Hills: California State College, 1967. **4**

Miles, Matthew B., ed. *Innovations in Education.* New York: Teachers College Press, 1964. **11**

Miller, G. A.; Galanter, E.; and Pribram, K. H. *Plans and the Structure of Behavior.* New York: Henry Holt, 1960. **3**

Miller, Richard I. *Education in a Changing Society.* Washington: National Education Association of the United States, Project on the Instructional Program of the Public Schools, 1964. **1**

Miller, Thomas E. *Educational Media In Instructional Systems Development at the Ohio State Univeristy.* Columbus: Research Foundation, Ohio State University, 1967. **5**

Milton, Ohmer. "Two-Year Follow-Up: Objective Data After Learning Without Class Attendance." *Psychological Reports* 11, December 1962, pp. 833–36. **14**

Mitzel, Harold E. *The Development and Presentation of Four College Courses by Computer Teleprocessing: Final Report.* University Park: Pennsylvaina State University, 1967. **7**

Molner, Don. "Micro-Teaching; Videotape Recording to Evaluate Teacher Training Performances." *Scholastic Teacher* 20, 7 March 1969, pp. 20–21; 25. **12**

Montgomery, Margaret A. "The Effects of Various Rates of Presentation in Combination with Massed and Spaced, Concurrent and Non-concurrent Practice Modes on Film Mediated Perceptual Motor Performance." Ph.D. dissertation, Indiana University, 1968. **10**

Morrill, Charles S. "Teaching Machines: A Review." *Psychological Bulletin* 58, September 1961, pp. 363–75. **6**

Morse, Dean, and Warner, Aaron W., eds. *Technological Innovation and Society: Columbia University Seminar on Technology and Social Change, 1965.* New York: Columbia University Press, 1966. **1**

Mundt, Allen V. "Toward Self Instruction Practice." *Audiovisual Instruction* 14, March 1969, pp. 86–88. **6**

Murray, Elwood, and Solomon, Arthur, eds. *The Student as Speaker and Listener.* Yellow Springs, Ohio: Antioch College and Jack Wolfram Foundation, 1966. **15**

Murray-Shelley, Richard. *Teach Yourself Computer Programming.* New York: Dover Publications, 1967. **7**

Naber, Richard H. "Dial for Education Information." *Audiovisual Instruction,* December 1968, pp. 1082–83. **5**

Naddor, Eliezer. "A Methodology for Computer-Aided Laboratories." *Journal of Engineering Education* 49, March 1969, pp. 858–60. **7**

Nash, Allan, and Adamson, Robert. "Effects of Information Feedback and Reference Tones on Signal Detection." *Psychonomic Science* 13, 25 December 1968, pp. 301–2. **10**

Neidt, Charles O. "Use of Videotaped Instructional Television for

Teaching Study Skills in a University Setting." *Audio Visual Communication Review* 15, Fall 1967, pp. 269–84. **8**

Neisser, U. "The Multiplicity of Thought." *British Journal of Psychology* 54 (1963) : 1–14. **3**

Nelson, Frank G. "Effects of Three Different Interaction Patterns on Programmed Learning Achievement." Ph.D. dissertation, Washington State University, 1968. **6**

Neumann, Eva. "Frequency and Usefulness of Verbal and Nonverbal Methods in the Learning and Transfer of a Paired-Associate Serial Motor Task." *Journal of Experimental Psychology* 60, August 1960, pp. 103–10. **3**

New Media Theory Conference: Working papers: "1–Structure and Function of Scientific Theories; 2–Learning Behavior Theory and Education; 3–Communication Theory and the Use of New Media; 4–Social Theory and the New Media; 5–Implication of Theory for Research." East Lansing: Michigan State University, March, 1962. **3**

The 1968 Catalog of Recorded Television Courses Available from National Great Plains Instructional Television Library. Lincoln: University of Nebraska. **8**

Nokes, Peter. "Feedback as an Explanatory Device in the Study of Certain Interpersonal and Institutional Processes." *Human Relations* 14, November 1961, pp. 381–87. **10**

Norberg, Kenneth, ed. "Perception Theory and Audio Visual Education." *Audio Visual Communication Review* 10 (1962) : 1–108. **3**

Oakes, W. F. "Use of Teaching Machines as a Study Aid in an Introductory Psychology Course." *Psychological Reports* 7 (1960) : 297–303. **6**

Oettinger, Anthony, and Marks, Sema. "Educational Technology: New Myths and Old Realities." *Harvard Educational Review* 38, Fall 1968, pp. 697–717. **1**

Ofiesh, Gabriel D., and Meierhenry, Wesley C., eds. *Trends in Programmed Instruction*. Washington: Department of Audiovisual Instruction, National Education Association and National Society for Programmed Instruction, 1964. **6**

One Week of Educational Television: Number Four: April 17–23, 1966. Waltham, Mass.: National Center for School and College Television, Brandeis University, Morse Communications Center, 1966. **8**

Ornstein, J. "Programed Instruction in the Language Field," *Education Digest* 34, February 1969, pp. 9–12. **13**

Osgood, C. A.; Suci, G. A.; and Tannenbaum, P. H. *The Measurement of Meaning*. Urbana: University of Illinois Press, 1957. **3**

Ostar, Allan W. *Relationships of Higher Education to National Policy: Assets and Liabilities*. Washington: American Association of State Colleges and Universities, 3 March 1968. **1**

Ott, Jack M. "Classification System for Decision Situations: An Aid to Educational Planning and Evaluation." *Educational Technology* 9 February 1969, pp. 20–23. **2**

"Our Not So Private Lives: Surveillance and Freedom." *Carnegie Corporation of New York: Quarterly Report 15*, Spring 1967. **15**

Oxhandler, Eugene K. "Can Subliminal Stimuli Teach?" *Audio Visual Communication Review* 8 (1960) : 109–14. **10**

Park, G., and Lewis, B. N. "An Adaptive Automation for Teaching Small Groups." *Perceptual Motor Skills* 14 (1962) : 183–88. **14**

Parker, Ralph. *A Feasibility Study for a Joint Computer Center for Five Washington, D. C., University Libraries*. Washington: Consortium of Universities of Metropolitan Washington, D. C., 1968. **7**

Pfau, Glen S. "Programed Instruction — An Exploration into its Effectiveness with the Handicapped Child." *Audiovisual Instruction*, November 1969, pp. 24–27. **6**

"Picturephone Utilizing Regular Voice-Grade Telephone Lines: Systems for Learning by Application of Technology to Education." *Newsletter*, Issue no. 10, July 1968, p. 3. **5**

Pinney, Robert H., and Miltz, Robert J. *Television Recordings and Teacher Education — New Directions*. Stanford, Calif.: Stanford University Center for Research and Development, November 1968. **8**

Poorman, Lawrence E. "A Comparative Study of the Effectiveness of a Multi-media System Approach to Harvard Project Physics with Traditional Approaches to Harvard Project Physics." Ph.D. dissertation, Indiana University, 1967. **13**

Popham, W. James. "Tape Recorded Lectures in the College Classroom," *Audio Visual Communication Review* 9, March–April 1961, pp. 109–18. **13**

Poulton, E. C. "Searching for Letters or Closed Shapes in Simulated Electronic Displays." *Journal of Applied Psychology* 52 (1968) : 348–56. **9**

President's Science Advisory Committee. *Computers in Higher Education*. Washington: U. S. Government Printing Office, 1967. **7**

Price, John F. *Television Facilities in Higher Education in New York State*. Albany, N. Y.: New York State Education Department, 1965. **8**

Professional Teacher Education: A Programmed Design by AACTE Teacher Education and Media Project. Washington: The American Association of Colleges for Teacher Education, 1968. **12**

Pryluck, C., and Snow, R. E. "Toward a Psycholinguistics of Cinema." *Audio Visual Communication Review* 15 (1967) : 54–75. **3**

Ramo, Simon. "The Computer as an Intellectual Tool." *The Information Revolution. The New York Times,* Sunday Supplement, 23 May 1965. **7**

Randall, Ronald K. "Perspectives on the 'Instructional System' " *Educational Technology* 9, February 1969, pp. 8–10. **1**

Rawls, James R.; Perry, Oliver; and Timmons, Edwin O. "A Comparative Study of Conventional Instruction and Individual Programmed Instruction in the College Classroom." *Journal of Applied Psychology* 50 (1966) : 388–91. **13**

Ray, Willis E. "Pupil Discovery vs. Direct Instruction." *Journal of Experimental Education* 29, March 1961, pp. 271–80. **15**

Resnick, L. B. "Programmed Instruction and the Teaching of Complex Intellectual Skills: Problems and Prospects." *Harvard Educational Review* 33 (1963) : 439–71. **6**

———. "Programmed Instruction and the Teaching of Social Studies Skills." *1963 Yearbook of the National Council for the Social Studies,* Washington, 1963, pp. 252–73. **6**

Rickover, H. G. *American Education: A National Failure.* New York: E. P. Dutton and Company, 1963. **1**

Riesman, David. *Constraint and Variety in American Higher Education.* Lincoln: University of Nebraska Press, 1965. **1**

Rigney, Joseph W., and Fry, Edward B. "Current Teaching-Machine Programs and Programming Techniques." *Audio Visual Communication Review* 9 (1961) : 122. **6**

Robertson, Lawrence M. "The Engineer-in-Training Examination and Registration." *Journal of Engineering Education* 59, March 1969, pp. 881–82. **12**

Roe, Arnold. "The ASEE Programmed Learning Project: Final Report." *Journal of Engineering Education* 59, March 1969, 62 pp. **6**

———. "Automated Teaching Methods Using Linear Programs." *Journal of Applied Psychology* 46, June 1962, pp. 198–201. **6**

———. "A Comparison of Branching Methods for Programmed Learning." *Journal of Educational Research* 55, June–July 1962, pp. 407–16. **6**

Roe, Arnold et al. *Automated Teaching Methods Using Linear Programs.* Los Angeles: University of Southern California, 1960. **6**

Rogers, C. R., and Skinner, B. F. "Some Issues Concerning the Control of Human Behavior—A Symposium." *Science* 124, 30 November 1956, pp. 1060–64. **3**

Rogers, E. M. *Diffusion of Innovation.* New York: Free Press, 1962. **11**

Root, Augustin A., coordinator. "Effective Teaching: Systems Approach to Instruction." *Journal of Engineering Education* 59, March 1969, pp. 835–82. **2**

Root, Augustin A. "Preview of Systems Approach to Instruction." *Journal of Engineering Education* 59, March 1969, p. 836. **2**

————. "Teaching as Decision Making." *Journal of Engineering Education* 59, March 1969, pp. 850–51. **3**

Rosenberg, Ronald C. "Computer Aided Teaching of Dynamic Systems Behavior." Washington: *USAF ESD Technical Report,* 1966. **7**

Rossi, Peter H., and Biddle, Bruce J., eds. *The New Media and Education: Their Impact on Society.* Chicago: Aldine Publishing Company, 1966. **4**

Rothkopf, Ernst Z. "Automated Teaching Devices and a Comparison of Two Variations of the Method of Adjusted Learning," *Psychology Report* 8 February 1961, pp. 163–69. **6**

————. "A Do-it-Yourself Kit for Programmed Instruction." *Teachers College Record* (1960) : 195–201. **6**

Roucek, Joseph S., ed. *Programmed Instruction: A Symposium on Automation in Education.* New York: Philosophical Library, 1965. **6**

Ryan, Paul. "Videotape and Special Education." *Audiovisual Instruction,* November 1969, pp. 30–31. **8**

Saettler, Paul. *History of Instructional Technology.* New York: McGraw-Hill Book Company, 1968. **1**

————. "Instructional Technology: Problems and Prospects." *Audio Visual Communication Review* 15, Summer 1967, pp. 133–44. **1**

Salomon, G., and Snow, R. E. *The Specification of Film Attributes* Self-Viewing One's Teaching Performance on Videotape." Paper presented at the annual convention of the American Psychological Association, San Francisco, August 1968. **10**

Salomon, G. and Snow, R. E. *The Specification of Film Attributes for Psychological and Educational Research Purposes.* Stanford University Center for Research and Development in Teaching, Research Memorandum no. 27, March, 1968. **8**

Scanlon, Robert G. "The Expansion of an Innovation." *Audiovisual Instruction,* November 1968, pp. 946–48. **11**

Schmookler, Jacob. *Invention and Economic Growth*. Cambridge, Mass.: Harvard University Press, 1966. **11**

Schrag, Peter. "Miami—Dade's Encounter with Technology." *Change* 1, March–April 1969, pp. 24–27. **13**

————. "The End of the Great Tradition." *Saturday Review*, 15 February 1969, pp. 94–96; 103–104. **1**

Schramm, W. *Programed Instruction Today and Tomorrow*. New York: Fund for the Advancement of Education, 1964. **6**

————. *Programed Instruction in Denver*. New York: Fund for the Advancement of Education, 1964. **7**

————. "What Do We Know About Learning from Instructional Television." *Educational Television: The Next Ten Years*. Stanford, Calif.: Institute for Communication Research, 1962. **8**

Schroder, Harold M.; Driver, Michael J.; and Streufert, Siegfried *Human Information Processing*. New York: Holt, Rinehart, and Winston, 1967. **3**

Schutz, Richard E. and Whittemore, Robert G., Jr. "Procedures for Giving Immediate Reinforcement in Programmed Instruction." *Journal of Experimental and Analytical Behavior* 5 (1962) : 541–42. **6**

Schwarg, G. "Computers in Physics Instruction." *Physics Today* 22, September 1969, pp. 41–49. **7**

Schwartz, Elizabeth. "The TV Studio as a Teaching Medium." *Audiovisual Instruction*, November 1969, pp. 60–66. **8**

Sebeok, T. A. "Coding in the Evolution of Signalling Behavior." *Behavioral Science* 8 (1962) : 430–42. **3**

Seidel, Robert Jo, and Rotberg, Iris C. "Effects of Written Verbalization and Timing of Information on Problem Solving in Programed Learning." *Journal of Educational Psychology* 57 (1966) : 151–58. **6**

Sessions, Frank Q., and Carruth, Max L. "Student Performance in Morning and Afternoon Classes." *Personnel and Guidance Journal* 4 (1962) : 144–46. **15**

Severin, W. J. "The Effectiveness of Relevant Pictures in Multiple-Channel Communications." *Audio Visual Communication Review* 15 (1967) : 386–401. **3**

————. "Another Look at Cue Summation." *Audio Visual Communication Review* 15 (1967) : 233–45. **3**

Sharp, Carleton B. "Relationship of Intelligence to Step Size on a Teaching Machine Program." *Journal of Educational Psychology* 52 (1961) : 98–103. **6**

Sharp, Stanley. "Architectural Steps in Facilities Planning." *Audio-visual Instruction,* February 1965, pp. 101–3. **14**

Sherburne, E. G. "ETV Research in the Decade Ahead." *Audio Visual Communication Review* 8 (1960) : 192–201. **3**

Sherman, Mark A. "The Relation of Posttest Performance to Response-Contingencies in Programmed Instruction." *USAF ESD Technical Report* 65 (1965) : 7. **10**

Shoemaker, Harry A. "The Functional Context Method of Instruction." *IRE Transactions on Education, E-III,* June 1960, pp. 52–57. **3**

Shultz, Morton J. *The Teacher and Overhead Projection.* Englewood Cliffs, N. J.: Prentice-Hall, 1965. **8**

Siegel, Laurence. "The Instructional Gestalt: A Conceptual Framework." *Teachers College Record* 62 (1960) : 202–13. **3**

Siegel, Laurence; Adams, James F.; and Macomber, F. G. "Retention of Subject Matter as a Function of Large Group Instructional Procedures." *Journal of Educational Psychology* 51, February 1960, pp. 9–13. **10**

Silberman, Charles E. "The Remaking of American Education." *Fortune,* April 1961, pp. 3–11. **1**

Silberman, Harry F. "A Computer as an Experimental Laboratory Machine for Research on Automated Teaching Procedures." *Behavioral Science* 5 (1960) : 175–76. **7**

———. "Self-Teaching Devices and Programmed Materials." *Review of Educational Research* 32, April 1962, pp. 179–93. **6**

Silberman, Harry F.; Melaragno, R. J.; Coulson, J. E.; Estavan, D. P. "Fixed Sequence vs. Branching, Auto-Instructional Methods." *Journal of Educational Psychology* 62 (1962) : 156–72. **6**

Silverman, Robert E., and Alter, Millicent. "Notes on the Response in Teaching Machine Programs." *Psychological Reports* 7 (1960) : 496. **6**

Silvern, L. C. "Cybernetics and Education K-12." *Audiovisual Instruction* 13 (1968) : 267–75. **2**

Skinner, B. F. "The Science of Learning and the Art of Teaching." In *Cumulative Record,* New York: Appleton-Century-Crofts, 1961. **3**

———. "Reflections on a Decade of Teaching Machines." *Teachers College Record* 65 (1963) : 168–77. **6**

———. "Teaching Machines." *Scientific American* 5 (1961) : 90–107. **6**

———. *The Technology of Teaching.* New York: Appleton-Century-Crofts, 1968. **3**

————. "Why We Need Teaching Machines." *Harvard Educational Review* 31 (1961) : 378–98. **6**

Sleeman, Phillip J., and Goff, Robert. "The Instructional Materials Center: Dialogue or Discord?" *Audio Visual Communication Review* 15 Summer 1967, pp. 160–68. **5**

Smith, Daniel M.; Schagrin, Morton; and Poorman, L. Eugene. "Multimedia Systems: A Review and Report of a Pilot Project." *Audiovisual Communication Review* 15, Winter 1967, pp. 345–69. **2**

Smith, Norman H. "The Teaching of Elementary Statistics by the Conventional Classroom Method Versus the Method of Programmed Instruction." *Journal of Educational Research* 55, June–July 1962, pp. 417–20. **6**

Smith, Robert D. "Simulation of a Psychological Decision Process: A Heuristic Approach." *Dissertation Abstracts A,* vol. 27, pp. 2696–97. Ann Arbor, Mich.: University Microfilms, 1967. **9**

Snow, C. P. "Miasma, Darkness, and Torpidity." *New Statesman* 42 (1961) : 186. **1**

Snow, R. E.; Tiffin, J.; and Seibert, W. E. "Individual Differences and Instructional Film Effects." *Journal of Educational Psychology* 56 (1965) : 315–26. **8**

Sommer, Robert. *Personal Space.* Englewood Cliffs, N. J.: Prentice-Hall, 1969. **14**

Standlee, Lloyd S., and Popham, W. James. "Quizzes' Contribution to Learning." *Journal of Educational Psychology* 51, December 1960, pp. 322–25. **3**

Stewart, William A. C., and McCann, W. P. *Educational Innovators.* New York: St. Martin's Press, 1967. **11**

Stolurow, Lawrence M. "Implications of Current Research and Future Trends." *Journal of Educational Research* 55 (1962) : 519–527. **3**

Stone, J. Blair. "The Effects of Learner Characteristics on Performance in Programed Text and Conventional Text Formats." *Journal of Educational Research* 59 (1965) : 122–27. **15**

Stovall, Gayden F. "Long Distance Learning." *Audiovisual Instruction,* February 1969, pp. 20–23. **4**

Srygley, Sara Kerntzman. "The Making of New School Media Specialists—From the Library Point of View." *Audiovisual Instruction,* January 1969, pp. 15–19. **15**

Suedfeld, P., and Streufert, S. "Information Search as a Function of Conceptual and Environmental Complexity." *Psychonomic Science* 4 (1966) : 351–52. **3**

Suppes, Patrick. "Computer Based Instruction: The Role of Computers in the Classroom of Tomorrow." *Electronic Age,* Summer 1967, pp. 2–6 **7**

———. "Defense of Computer Assisted Instruction in Russian." *Harvard Educational Review,* Fall 1968, p. 735. **7**

———. "The Use of Computers in Education." *Scientific American,* vol. 215, no. 3, September 1966, pp. 206–8; 213–20. **7**

Suppes, Patrick and Jerman, Max. "Computer Assisted Instruction at Stanford." *Educational Technology,* January 1969, pp. 22–24. **7**

Swets, John; Harris, Judith R.; McElroy, Linda S.; and Rudloe, Harry. "Computer-Aided Instruction in Perceptual Identification." *Behavioral Science* 11 (1966) : 98–104. **7**

Symposium: A Systems Approach to Curricular and Instructional Planning. American Educational Research Association annual meeting, Chicago, 1968. **2**

Taft, Martin I. "A Systematic Method for Evaluating Teachers." *Journal of Engineering Education* 59, March 1969, pp. 852–57. **15**

Tanner, C. Kenneth. "Educational Systems Analysis." *Audiovisual Instruction* 14, March 1969, pp. 89–91. **2**

Taylor, C. W. and Williams, F. E. *Instructional Media and Creativity.* New York: John Wiley and Sons, 1966. **11**

"Teaching Machine for Drama." Birmingham-Southern College, Alabama. *Architectural Forum* 130, Spring 1969, pp. 78–83. **6**

Television and Education: A Bibliography. New York: Television Information Office, 1960. **2**

Television for Higher Education in Colorado—A Five Year Plan. Denver: Association of State Institutes of Higher Education in Colorado, 1964. **8**

Terrace, H. S. "Discrimination Learning with and without Errors." Ph.D. dissertation, Harvard University, 1960. **3**

Thomas, Squadron Leader C. A.; Davies, Squadron Leader I. K.; Openshaw, Flight Lieutenant D.; and Bird, Flight Lieutenant J. B. *Programmed Learning in Perspective: A Guide to Programme Writing.* London: City Publicity Services, for Lamson Technical Products, 1963. **6**

Tiemann, Philip W. "Outcomes in a Televised College Economics Course with Variable Student Knowledge of Objectives." Ph.D. dissertation, University of Illinois, 1968. **10**

Time-Sharing System Scorecard, A Survey of On-line Multiple User Computer Systems. Newton, Mass.: Computer Research Corporation, 1967. **7**

Tinker, Miles A. "Devices to Improve Speed of Reading." *Reading Teacher* 20 (1967) : 605–09. **5**

Tobias, Sigmund. "Effect of Attitudes to Programed Instruction and other Media on Achievement from Programed Materials." *Audio Visual Communication Review* 17, Fall 1969, pp. 299–305. **15**

———. "Teaching Machines and Programed Instruction." *Audio Visual Communication Review* 14, Spring 1966, pp. 99–116. **6**

Travers, Robert M. W., ed. *Research and Theory Related to Audiovisual Information Transmission.* Salt Lake City: University of Utah, Bureau of Educational Research, Interim Report, 1964. **3**

Trow, William C. *Teacher and Technology—New Designs for Learning.* New York: Appleton-Century-Crofts, 1963. **1**

Traxler, Arthur E., ed. *Innovation and Experiment in Modern Education.* Washington: American Council on Education, 1965. **11**

Twyford, Loran C., Jr. "New Directions for Research in the 1970's" *Audiovisual Instruction* 13, June–July 1968, pp. 590–92. **3**

Tyler, Louise L. "The Taxonomy of Educational Objectives: Cognitive Domain—Its Use in Evaluating Programmed Instruction." *California Journal of Educational Research* 17 (1966) : 26–32. **6**

Undergraduate Experience Abroad (1957–61). Yellow Springs, Ohio: Antioch College, April 1968. **14**

Ushkow, Elliott A. "The Influence of Criterion Text Type and the Amount of Delay between Learning and Testing on the Effectiveness of Overt and Non-Overt Responding to Programmed Instruction." Ph.D. dissertation, New York University, 1967. **10**

Van Cott, Harold P., and Kinkade, Robert G. "Human Simulation Applied to the Functional Design of Information Systems." *Human Factors* 10 (1968) : 211–16. **9**

Van Mondfrans, A., and Travers, R. M. "Learning of Redundant Material Presented Through Two Sensory Modalities." *Perceptual and Motor Skills* 19 (1964) : 743–51. **3**

Veldman, Donald J. *Computer-Based Sentence-Completion Interviews.* Austin: University of Texas, 1967.

Vento, Charles J. "A Media Distribution System of the Future." *Audiovisual Instruction,* December 1968, pp. 1078–81. **5**

Verduin, John R., Jr. *Conceptual Models in Teacher Education: An Approach to Teaching and Learning.* Washington: American Association of Colleges for Teacher Education, 1967. **9**

Vidale, Richard F. "Some Cautions in Applying Systems Analysis to Education." *Journal of Engineering Education* 59, March 1969, pp. 837–40. **2**

Wales, Charles E. "Programmed Instruction Closes Two Generation

Gaps." *Journal of Engineering Education* 59, March 1969, pp. 866–68. **6**

———. "Educational Systems Design." *Journal of Engineering Education* 59, March 1969, pp. 866–68. **2**

Walker, Eric A. "The Next One Hundred Years." An address on the Occasion of the Centennial Convocation at Clarion State College, 1 May 1968. **1**

Wartenberg, Milton, ed. "Introduction: How One School System Uses Media." *Audiovisual Instruction* 14, May 1969, pp. 17–46. **5**

Watson, Paul G. "Instructional Strategies and Learning Systems." *Audiovisual Instruction,* vol. 13, no. 8, October 1968, pp. 842–46. **2**

Wedemeyer, C. A. "New Uses for the 'Tools' of Education." *The NUEA Spectator* 30, April–May 1965, pp. 14–19. **4**

Weisgerber, Robert A., ed. *Instructional Process and Media Innovation.* Chicago: Rand McNally and Company, 1969. **11**

Weisgerber, Robert A., and Rahmlow, Harold F. "Individually Managed Learning." *Audiovisual Instruction,* October 1968, pp. 835–39. **6**

Wendt, Paul R., and Butts, Gordon K. "Audio-visual Materials." *Review of Educational Research* 32, April 1962, pp. 141–55. **3**

Wendt, Paul R., and Rust, Grosvenor. "Pictorial and Performance Frames in Branching Programmed Instruction." *Journal of Educational Research* 55, June–July 1962, pp. 430–32. **6**

Wiley, John, and Sons. *Guide for Wiley Authors in the Preparation of Linear Auto-Instructional Programs.* New York: John Wiley and Sons, 1967. **6**

Wilhelmsen, Frederick D., and Bret, Jane. *Media, Machines, and Man.* Athens, Ga.: University of Georgia Press, 1969. **4**

Williams, B. "Freelance Job Idea: Writing Programmed Instruction Materials." *Writers Digest* 49, September 1969, pp. 36–42. **12**

Williams, Joanna P. "Comparison of Several Response Modes in a Review Program." *Journal of Educational Psychology* 54 (1963): 253–60. **10**

Williams, Thomas G. and Frye, Charles H. "An Instructional Application of Computer Graphics." *Educational Technology,* June 1968, pp. 5–10. **7**

Wilsey, C. E. "Are You Ready For Your Own Data Processing Center?" *Education Digest* 34, January 1969, pp. 16–17. **7**

Winthrop, Henry. "What Can We Expect From the Unprogrammed Teacher?" *Teachers College Record* 67 (1966): 315–29. **15**

Witmer, David R. *The Computer as a Management Tool—Physical Facilities Inventories, Utilization, and Projections: 11th Annual Machine Records Conference Proceedings.* Knoxville: University of Tennessee, 1966. **7**

Woodward, John C. *Attitudes and Achievement Comparisons for Direct and Television Classes in Biological Science: Report 4.* Coral Gables, Fla.: University of Miami, July 1964. **8**

————. *Effect of Completely Permissive Attendance Regulations on Achievement and Attendance in Natural Science TV Lecture Course: Report 9.* Coral Gables, Fla.: University of Miami, January 1965. **8**

————. *The Effect of Immediate Feedback on Learning in Humanities: Report 7.* Coral Gables, Fla.: University of Miami, June 1964. **10**

————. *The Effect of Immediate Feedback on Learning in Social Science: Report 8.* Coral Gables, Fla.: University of Miami, September 1964. **10**

Woolman, Myron. *Programming for Conceptual Understanding.* A Report to the Communication Social Science Research Department of the Bell Telephone Laboratories. Washington: Institute of Educational Research, n.d. **6**

Worth, S. "Cognitive Aspects of Sequence in Visual Communication." *Audio Visual Communication Review* 16, Summer 1968, pp. 121–45. **3**

Wyman, Raymond. *The Instructional Materials Center—Whose Empire?* Washington: Department of Audiovisual Instruction, National Education Association, 1967. **5**

Zajac, E. E. "The Hourglass Instead of the Funnel in Educational Technology." *Educational Technology* 9, February 1969, pp. 28–29. **1**

index

Friends: a learning resource, 74
Furniture: grouping of chairs, 42

Gaps: between learners, 23
Genesys: University of Florida television program, 17
Grades: self-imposed, 28; as time limited, 63; as outputs, 93; pass/fail, 94
Grading: society's sieve, 7; authority of the teacher, 28; unpleasant associations, 94
Grid. *See* Matrix
Group dynamics: lever to learning improvement, 10

Harvard University: participant interaction, 87
Hidden agenda: its value in learning extraneous materials, 31
Higher education: its purpose, xvi
History class: preprogrammed materials, 61
Honor sections: enrichment potential, 87
Hopkins, Mark: student-teacher relationship, 34, 73
Hornbook: contrast with modern media, 73

Idea bank: need for storing concepts, 69
Idiosyncrasies: of teachers, 3, 88
Immediacy: in working with people, 64
Impersonality: deterrent to learning, 74
Inattention: hazard to class progress, 30
Incremental learning: estimates of, 91
Inner space: as a part of the environmental learning, 12
Innovations: by students and faculty, xv; involving technology, xvi; literature of, 117
Inputs: as a category, 15; matched with outputs, 15; received simultaneously, 17; saturation with lecture console feedback, 20; chart of, 21; clusters of, 71; ac-

cidental, 72; recycled, 72; level of use, 72; types of, 73; textbooks, 73; films, 73; records, 73; tapes, 73; computers, 73; calculators, 73; blackboards, 73; projectors, 73; telephone, 73; memory, 73; qualitative nature of, 73; rearrangements of, 75; as class-converted outputs, 76; by computer access, 76; world trip, exotic types, 77; rapid rise of, 77; problems with flooding passive response, 78; parameter of, 79
Insights: about total learning environment, 4; shared, 74
Instruction: modes of, 21; storage of materials, 68
Interaction: in learning, 1; levels of, 17; direction and kind, 21; people's effectiveness in, 32; nature of, 80; in lectures, 81; multi-level, 83; interference patterns, 83; complex visual signals, 85; creative use of, 86; screening device, 87; contribution to total experience, 87; parameter of, 88
Interplay: between students, 82
Isolation: in learning, 47

Jacobs, Philip: changing values, 96

Laboratory: defined, 53; sights and sounds as inputs, 75; evaluation of achievement, 93
Laminar flow: helps group learning, 30
Language: slow speed media, 68
Leadership: in learning, 54
Learners: junior and senior, 11, 23; involvement at three levels, 26
Learning: freedom to select learning materials, 86; latent effect of, 91; effect on peer group, 97; automation of, 103
Learning experience: dimensions of, xiii; defined, xvii; parameters described, 1; as an art, 3; effect of field trips, 26; research opportunities, 92; evaluation, 92;

79925

Television listening: while talking, 83

Tension: in learning, 18; as a teaching style, 74

Tests: defects in items, 65; as in input, 73

Textbooks: as an input, 71

Theories about learning: literature of, 110

Thorndike, Edward Lee: laws of learning, 5

Time: modes defined, 14; mixed mode, 14, 67; real-time mode, 14; time-bending mode, 62; mode in memory, 63; mode related to purpose, 63; acceptance of non-real-time mode, 66; plausible reality, 66; advantages of non-real-time mode, 67; intermix for review purposes, 67; in future mode, 69; lag shortened with media, 69; displacement in social orientation, 70

Titles: for teachers, 28

Toastmaster's clubs: as effective self-teaching, 57

Transference. *See* Feedback; Interaction

Transmission: one and two-way, 16

Tutor: role of mediator, 28

Tutorials: pattern of, 100

University: medieval model, xiv; task defined, xviii

Values: changes in college, 96

Video tape: as deferred lectures, 62

Visual ability: prolific receptor, 86

Visuals: affecting rapport, 55

Visual signals: response by students, 68; as stored symbols, 82

Vocational relationships: literature of, 118

Voluntary learning: popular style, 57

Whole man: his development, 98

Wire service: as an input, 76

Worlds fair: New York's use of capsules, 37